DESERT MUSE
COLORING BOOK

I0489632

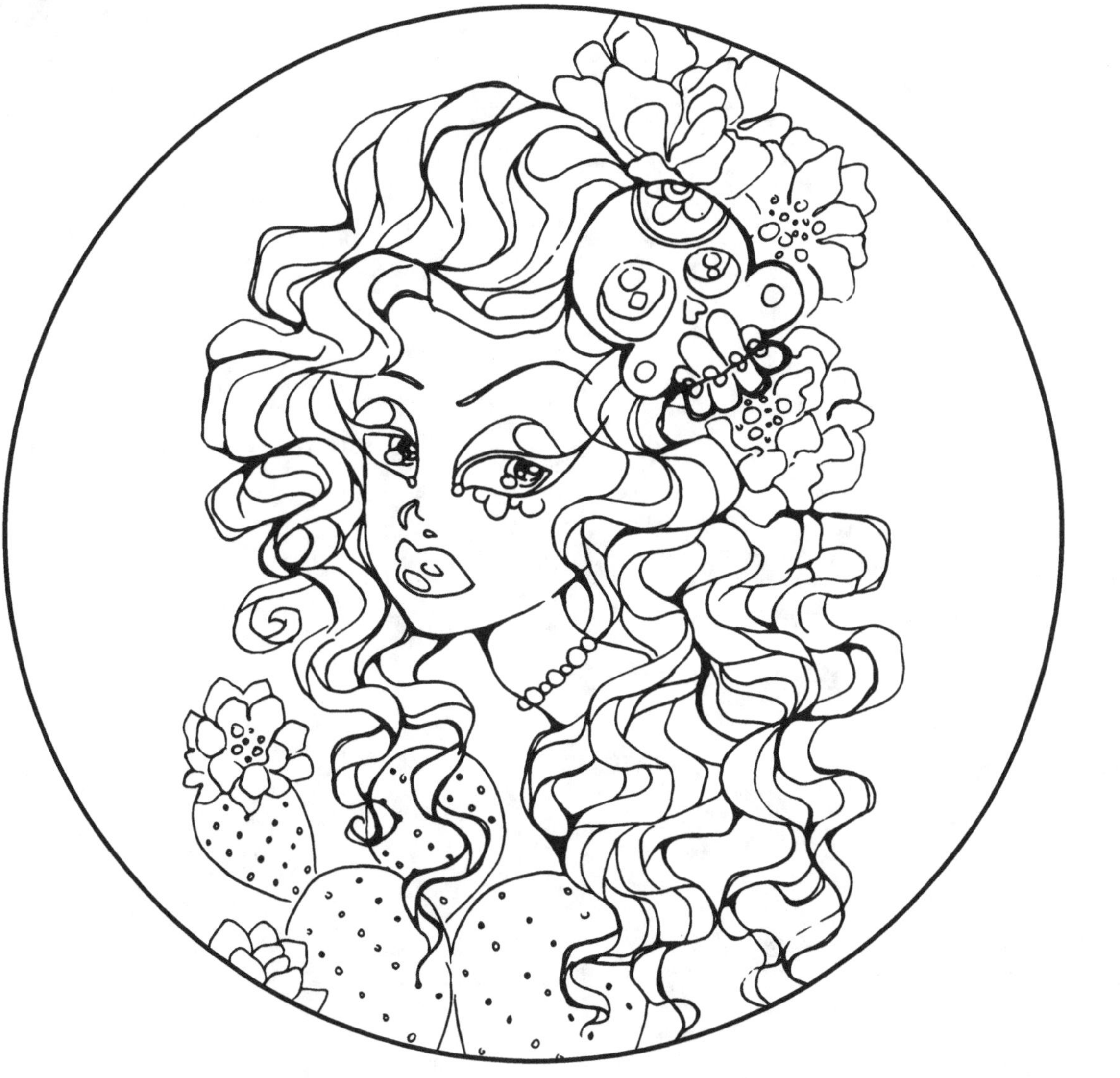

illustrated by KARLA MAGAÑA

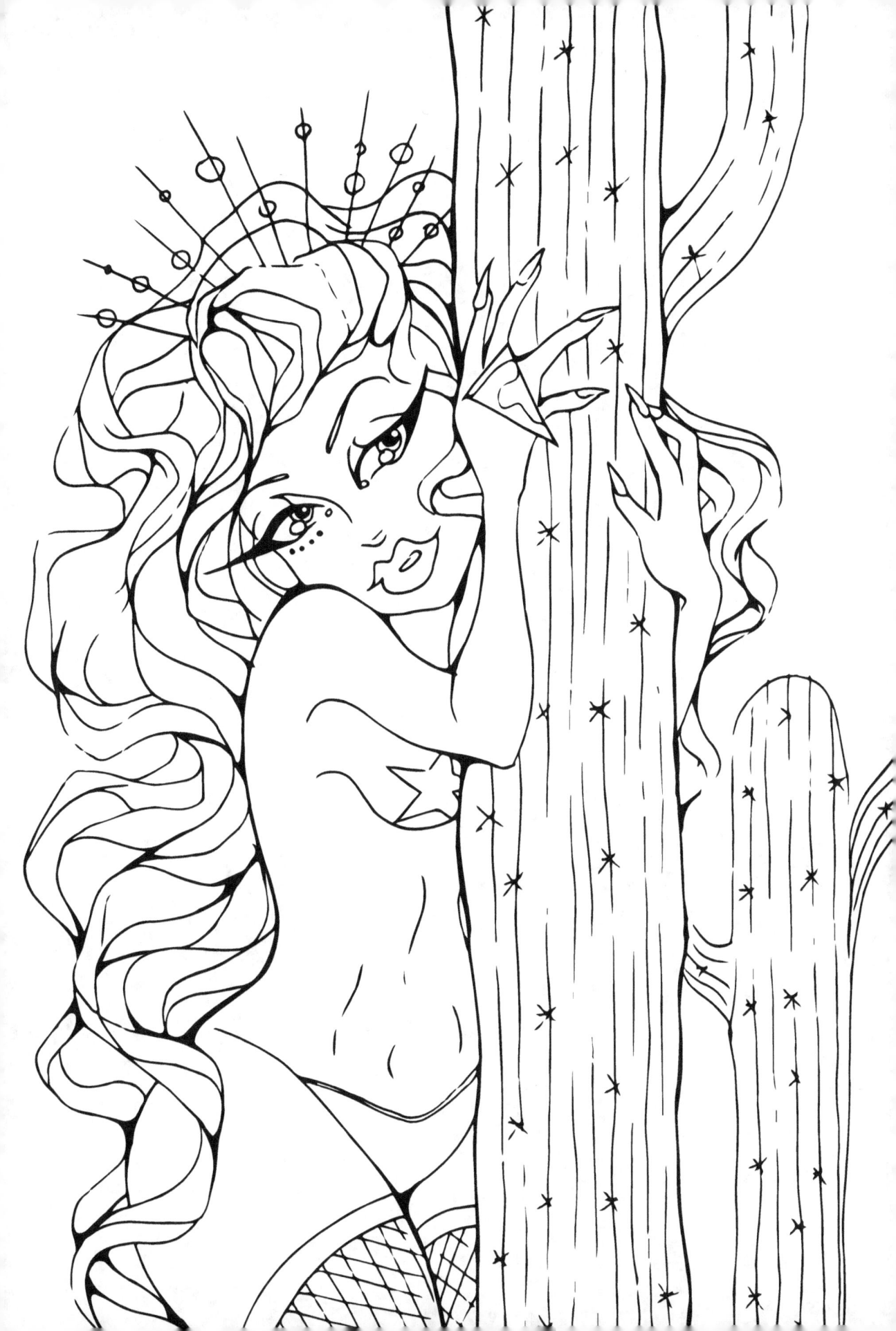

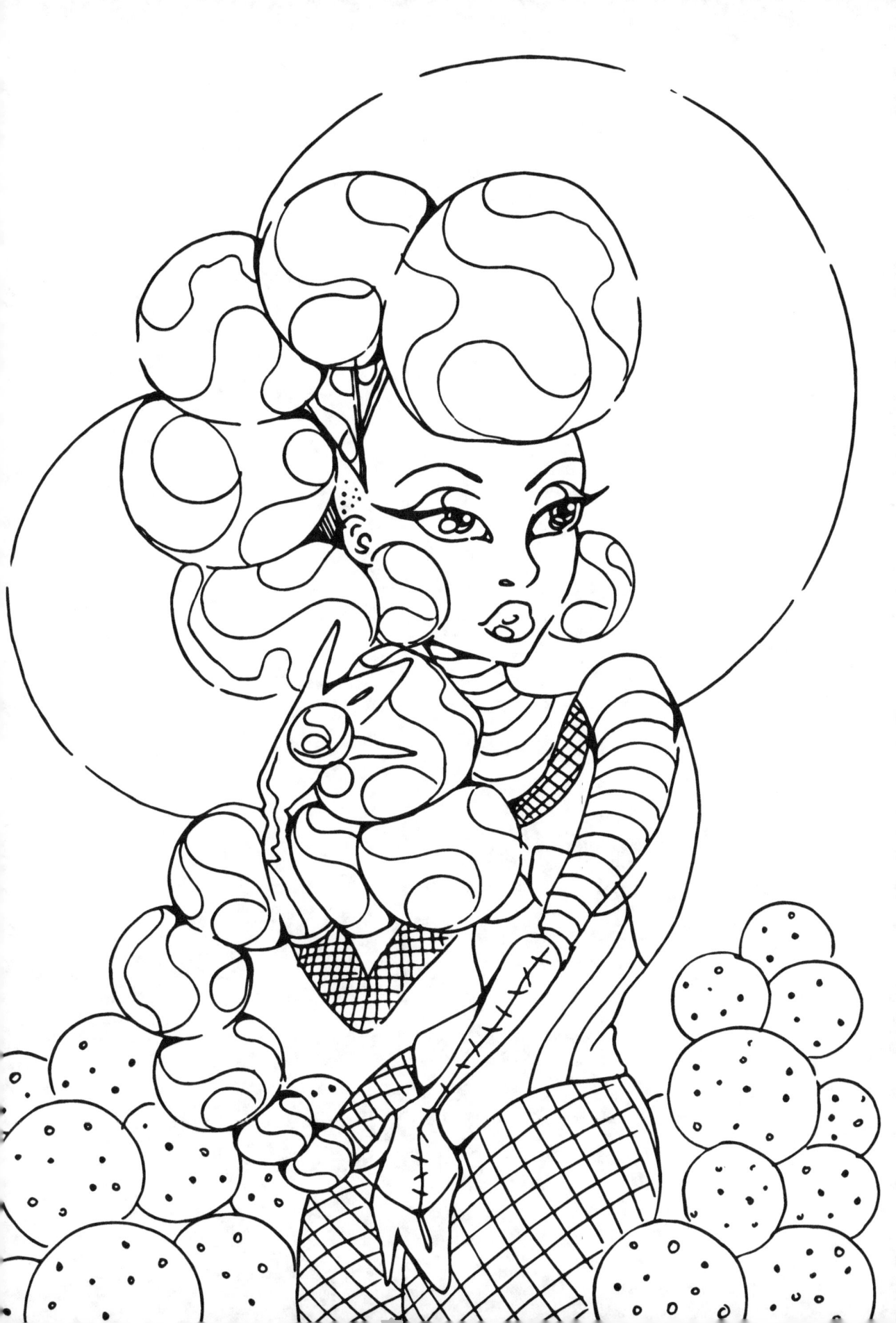

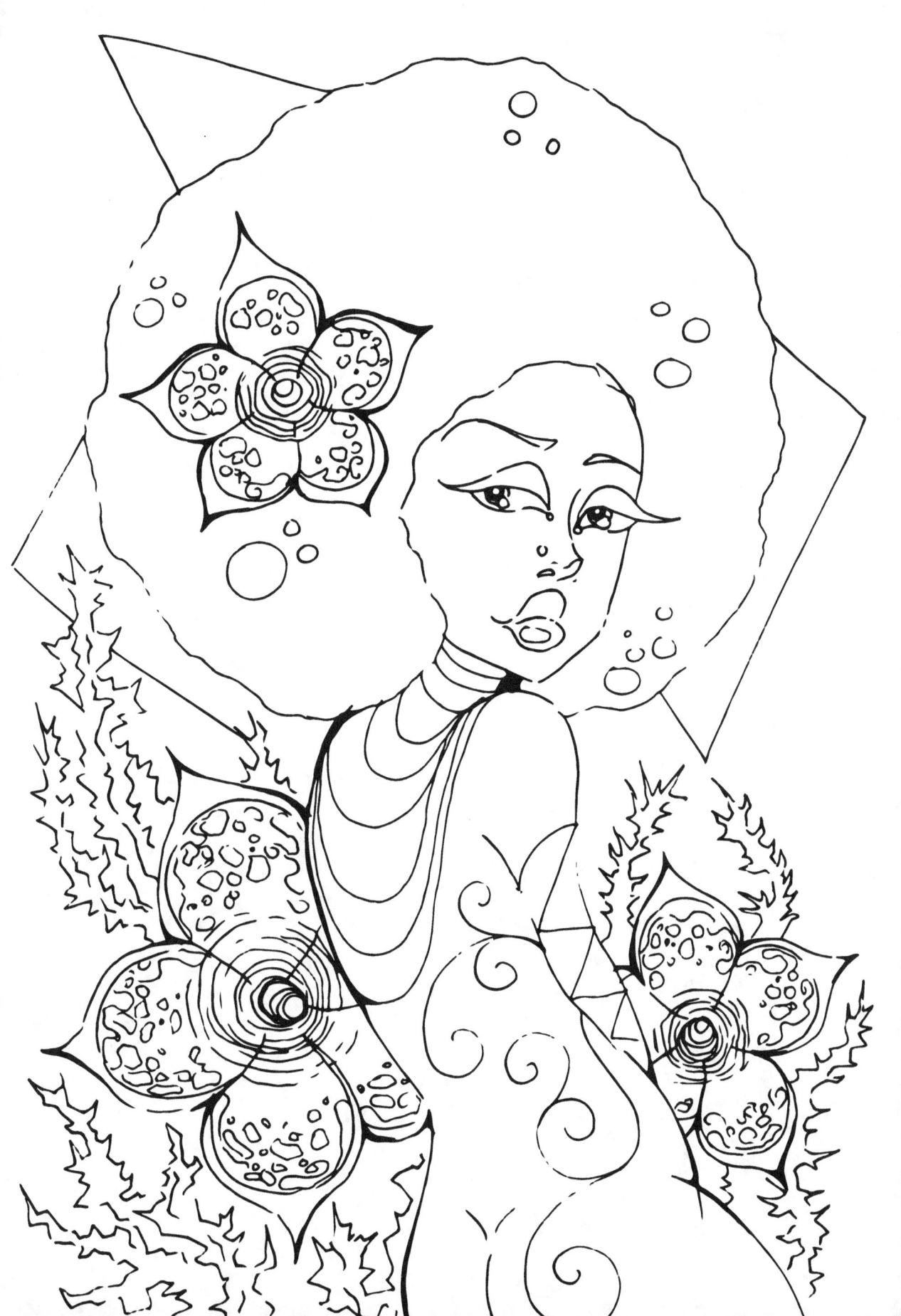

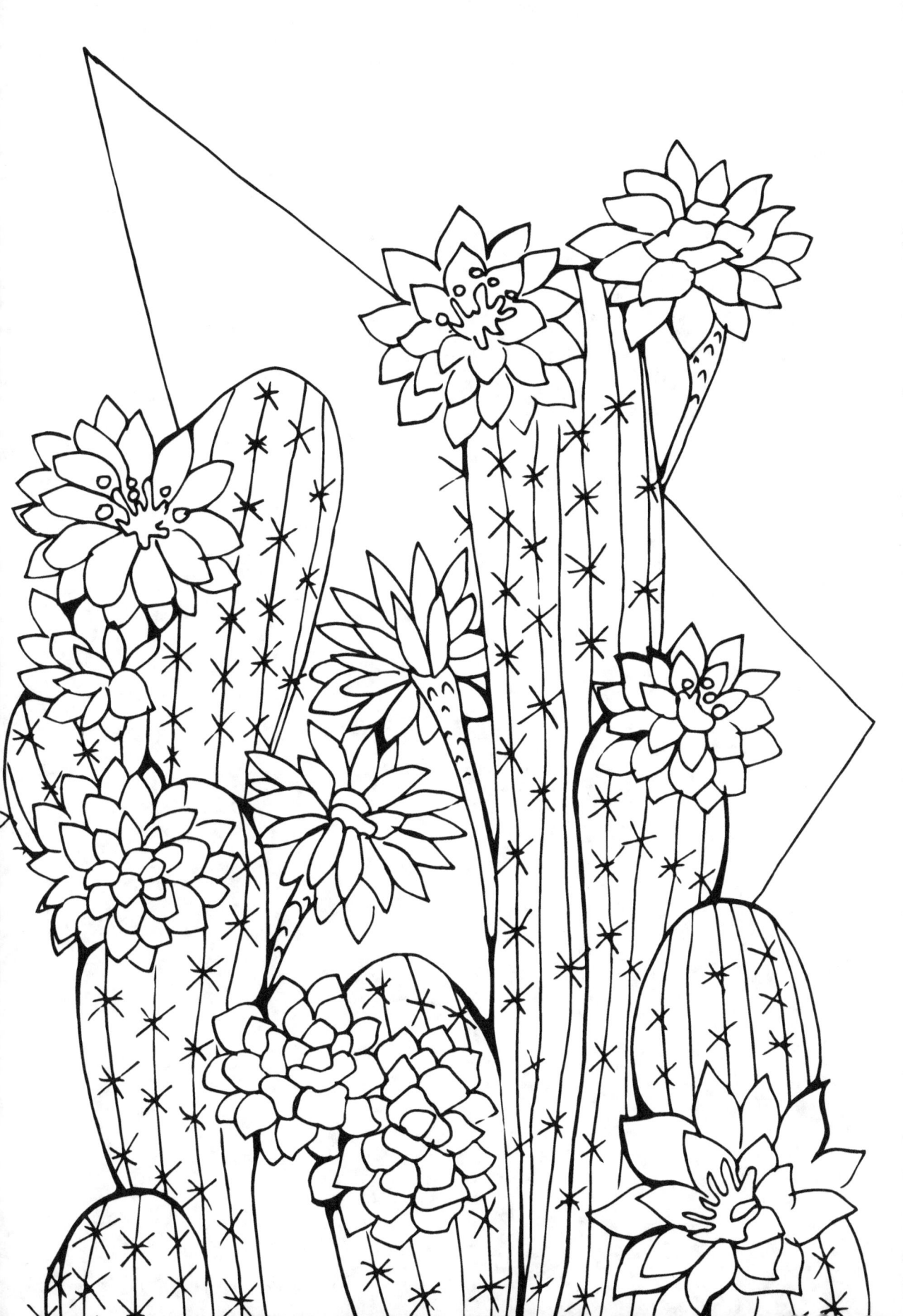

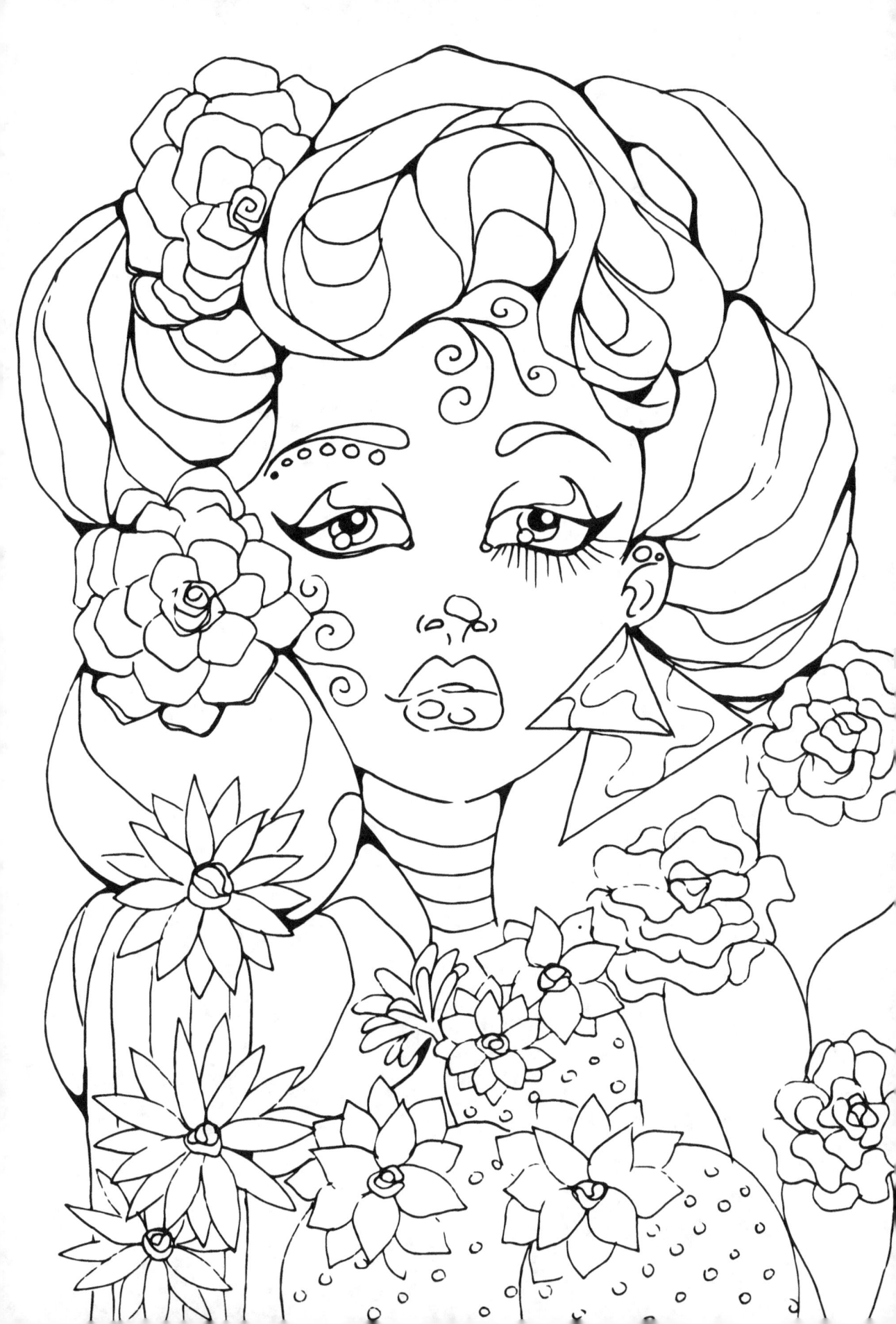

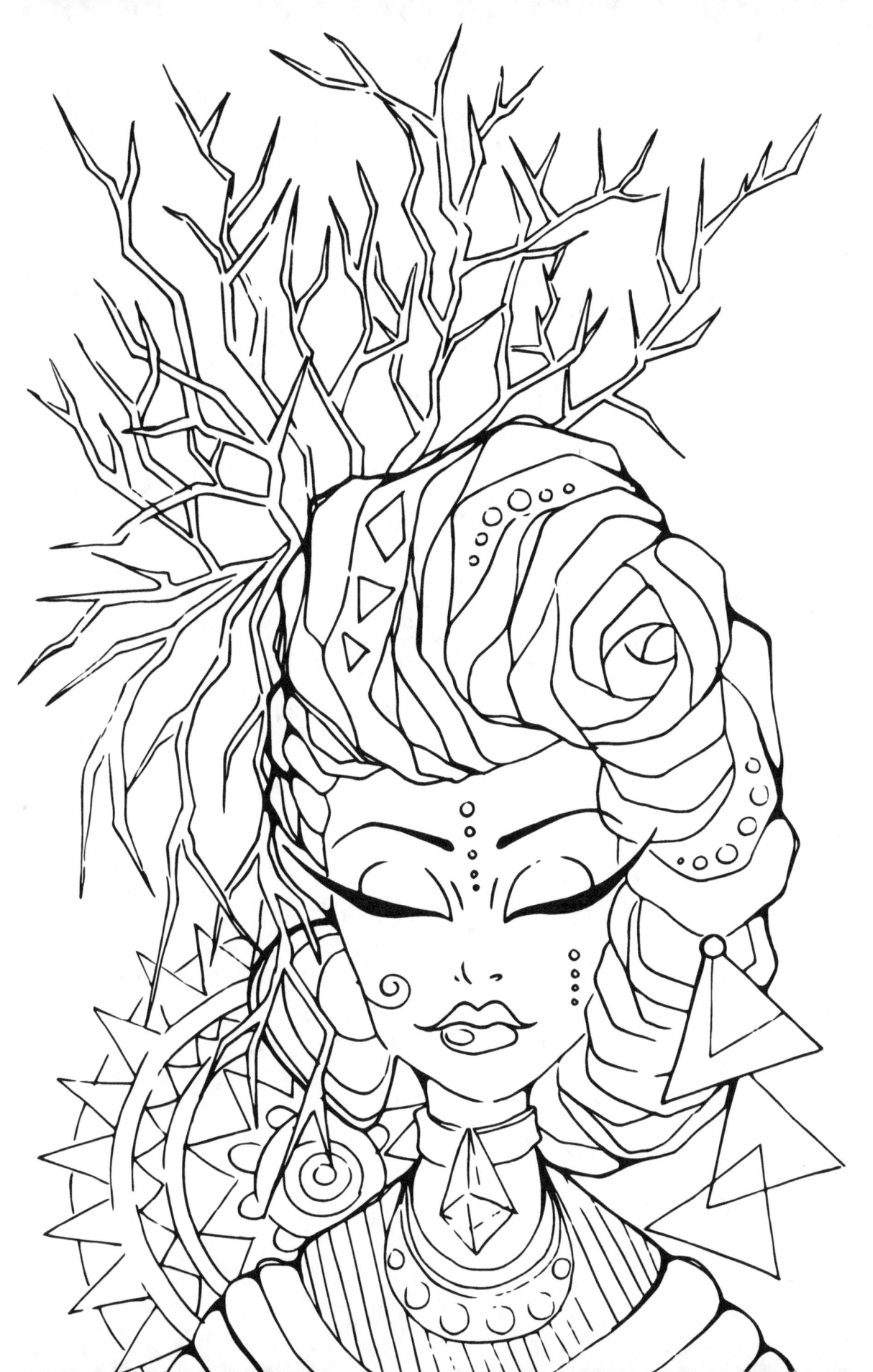

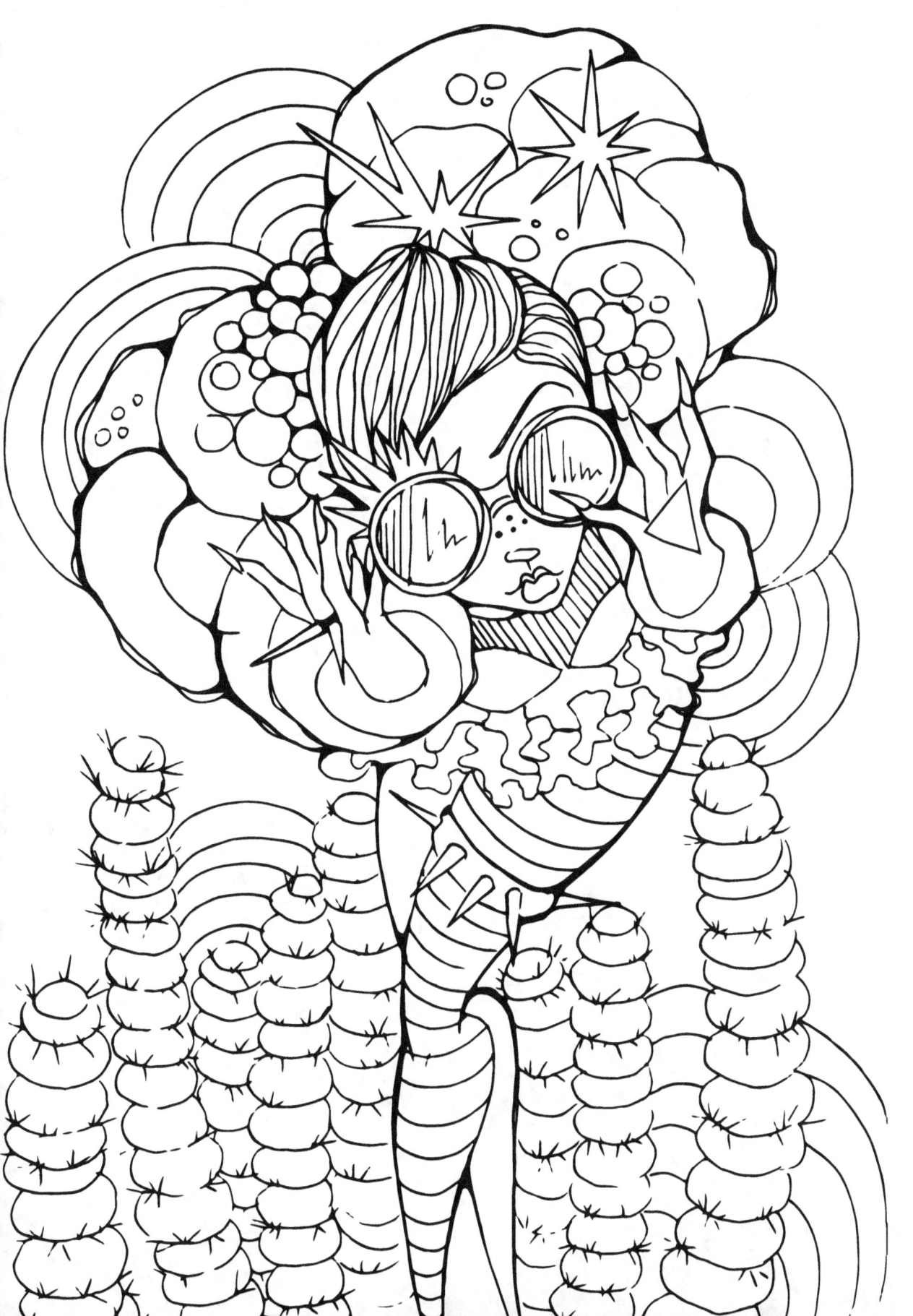

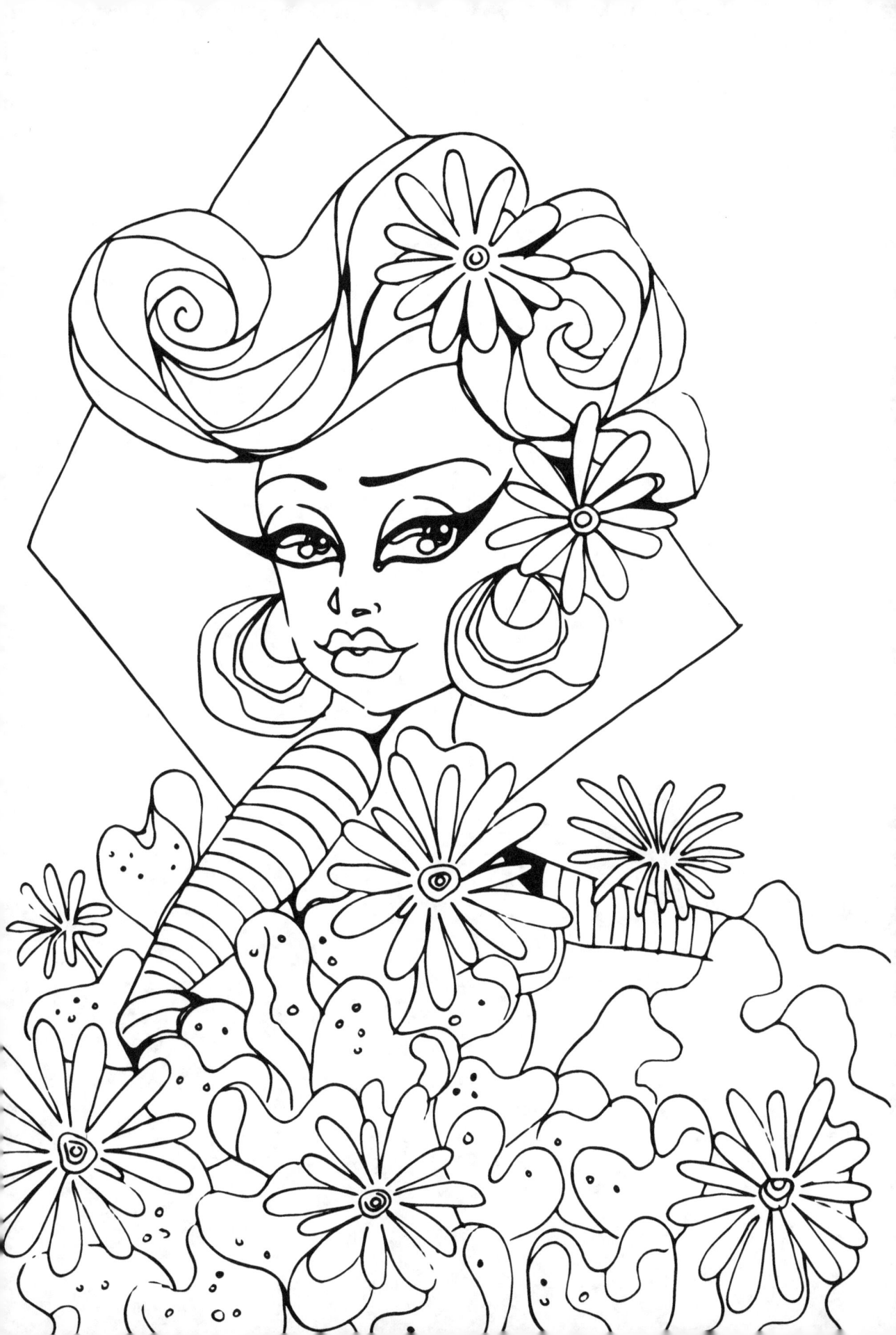

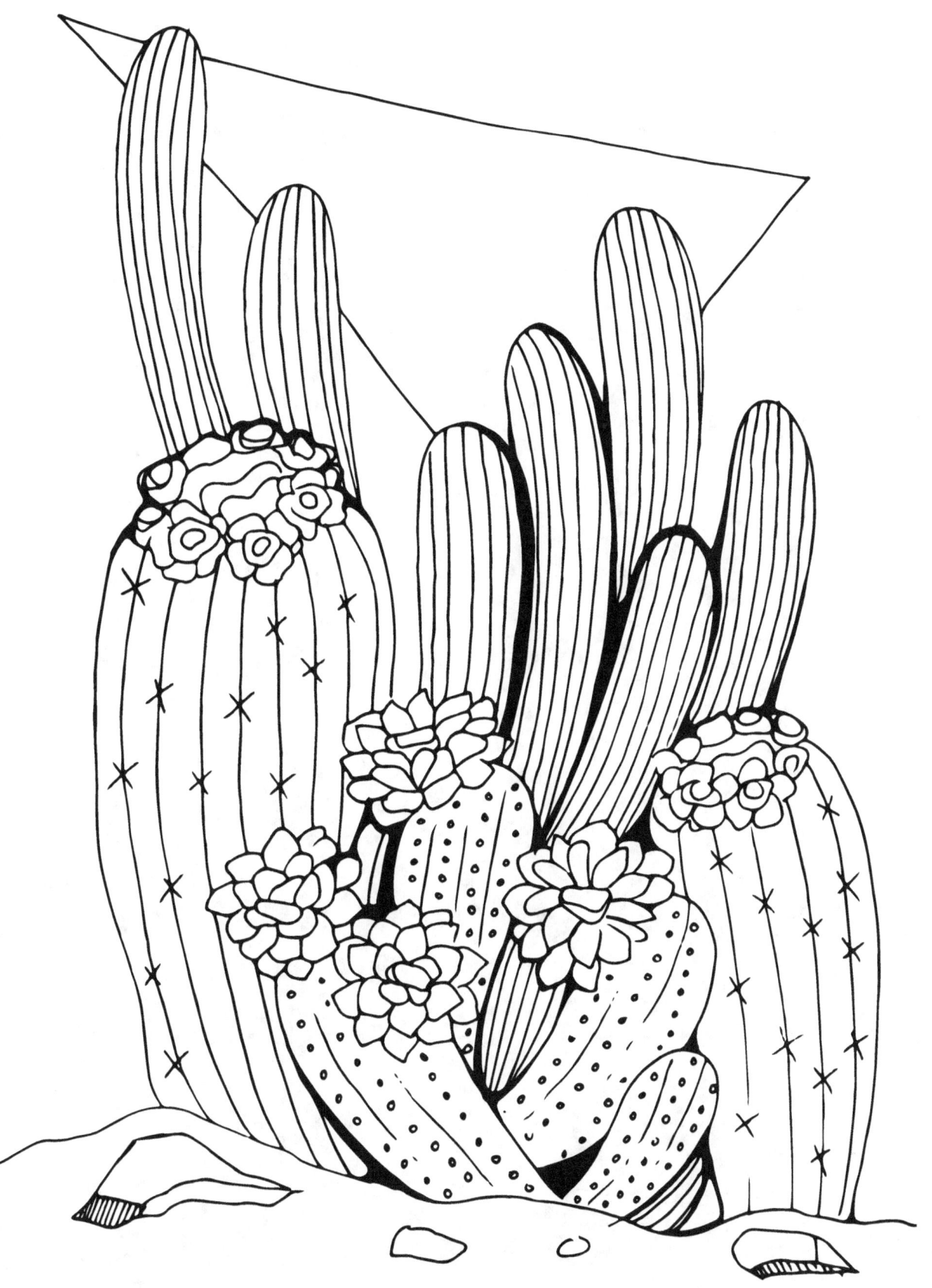

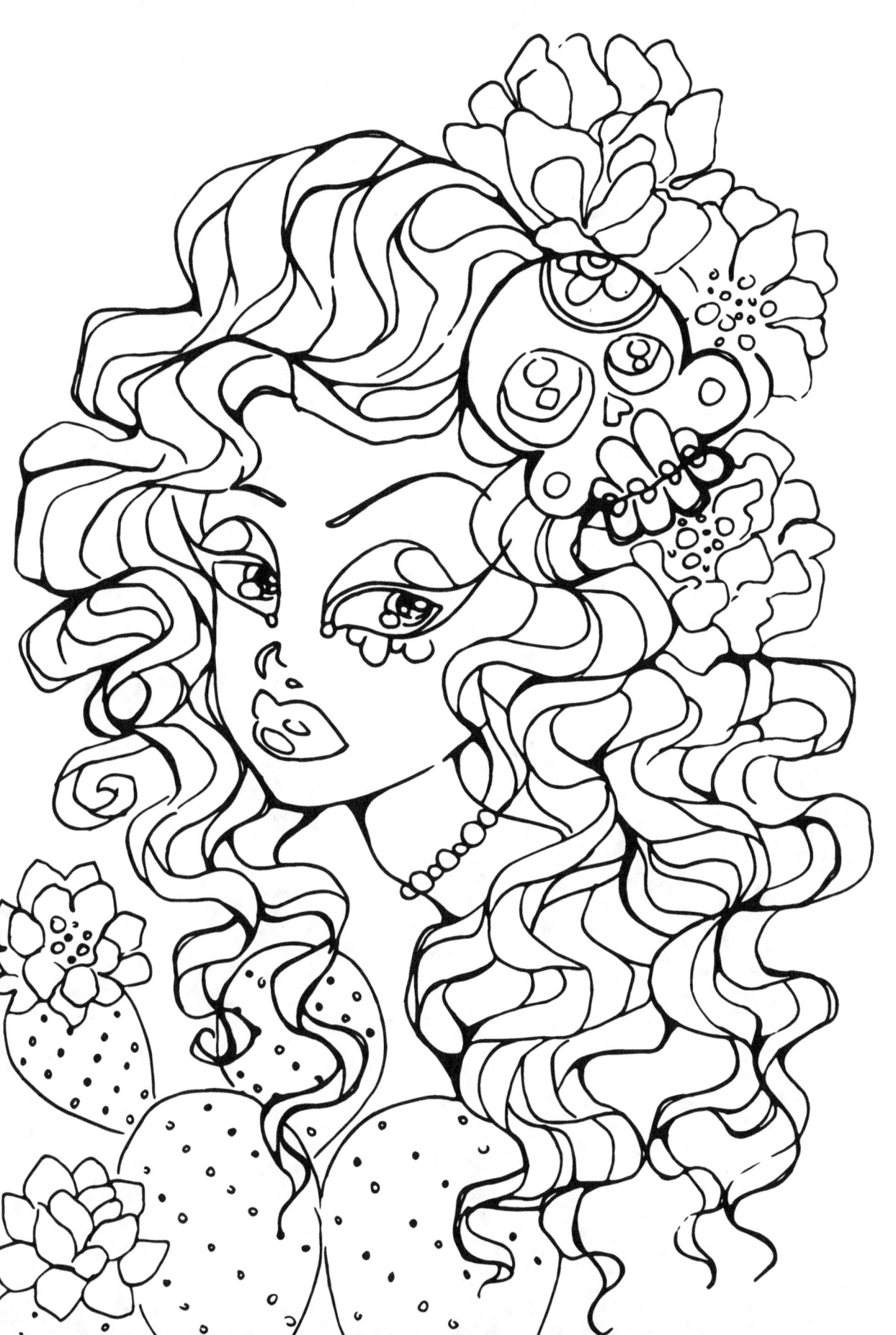

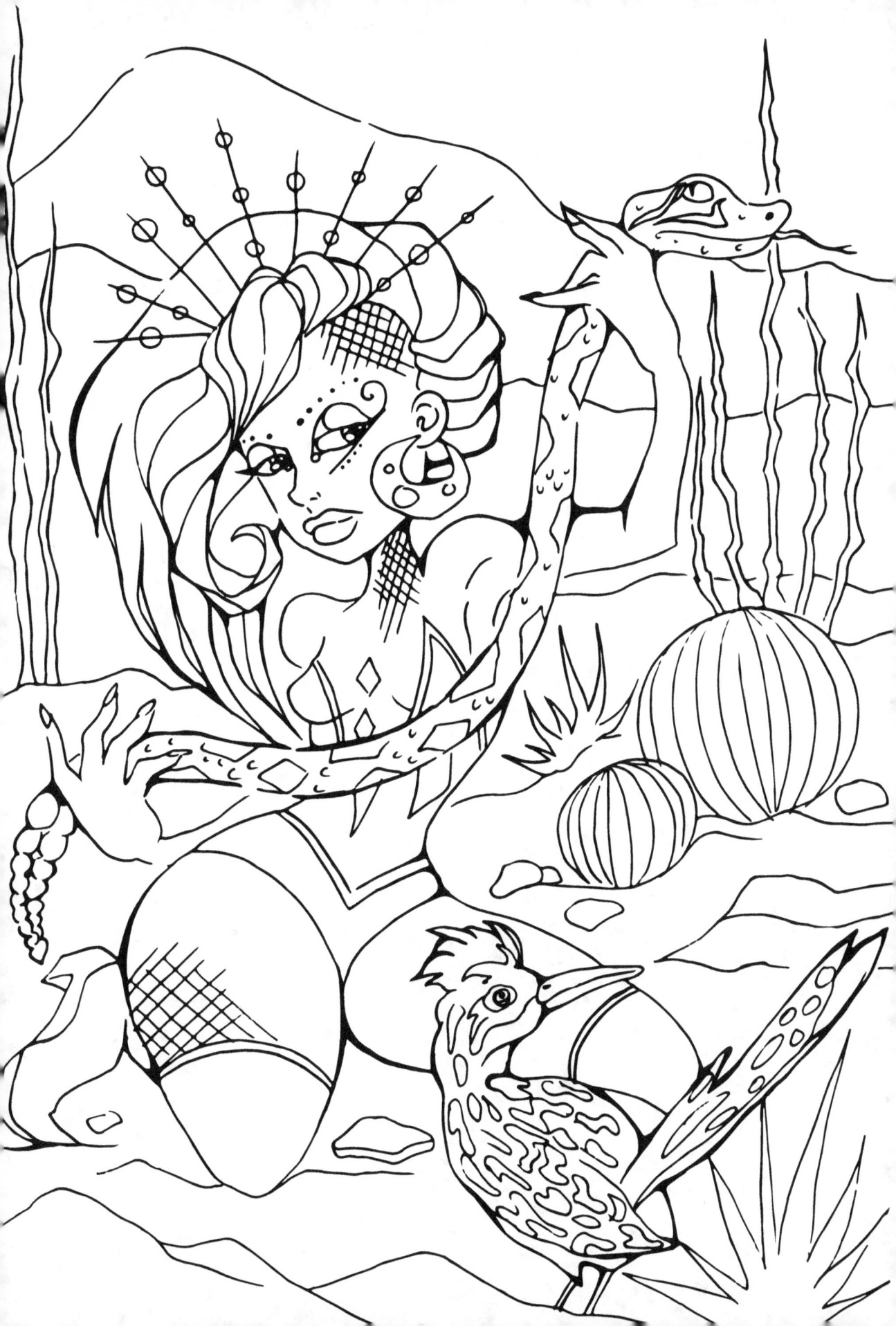

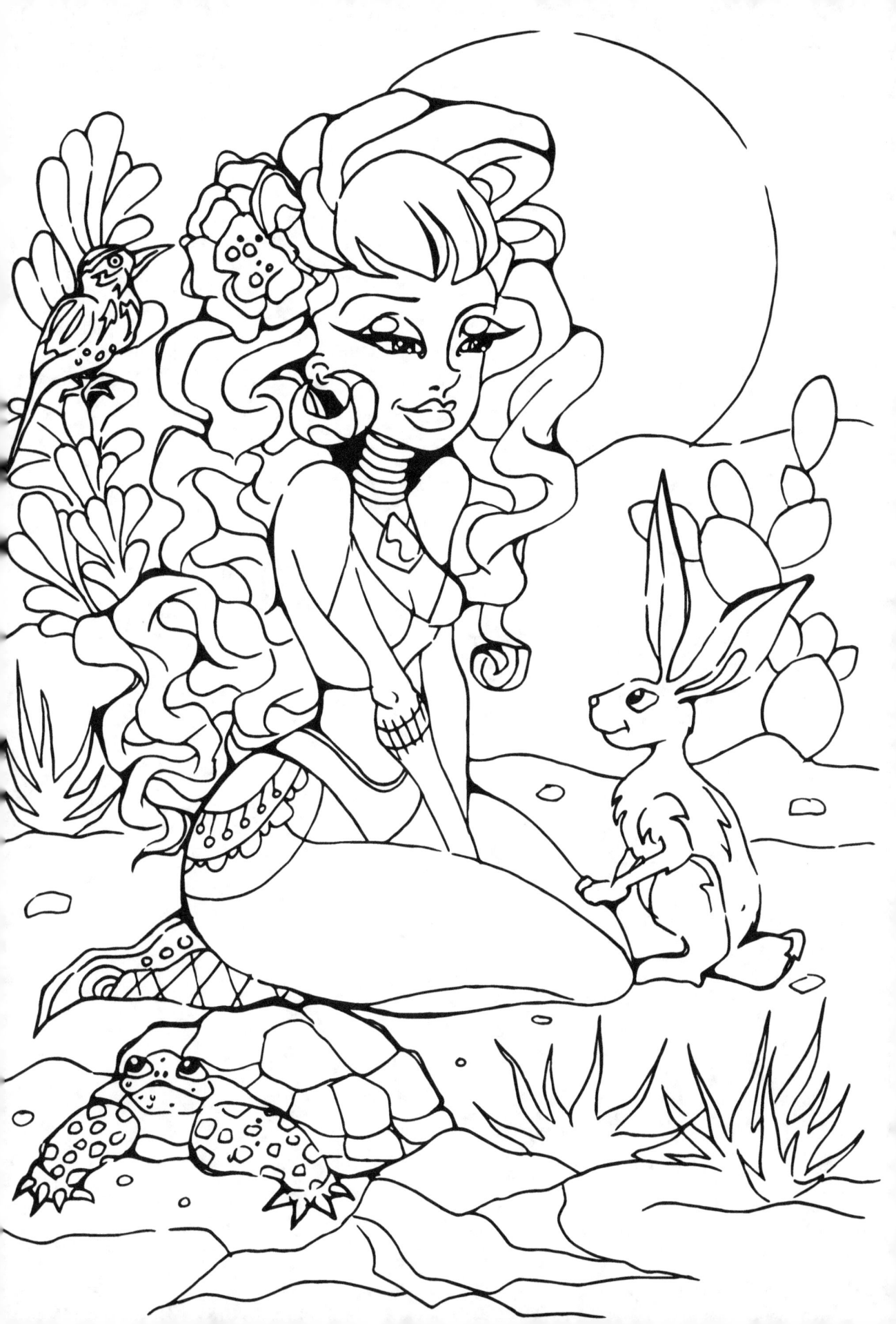

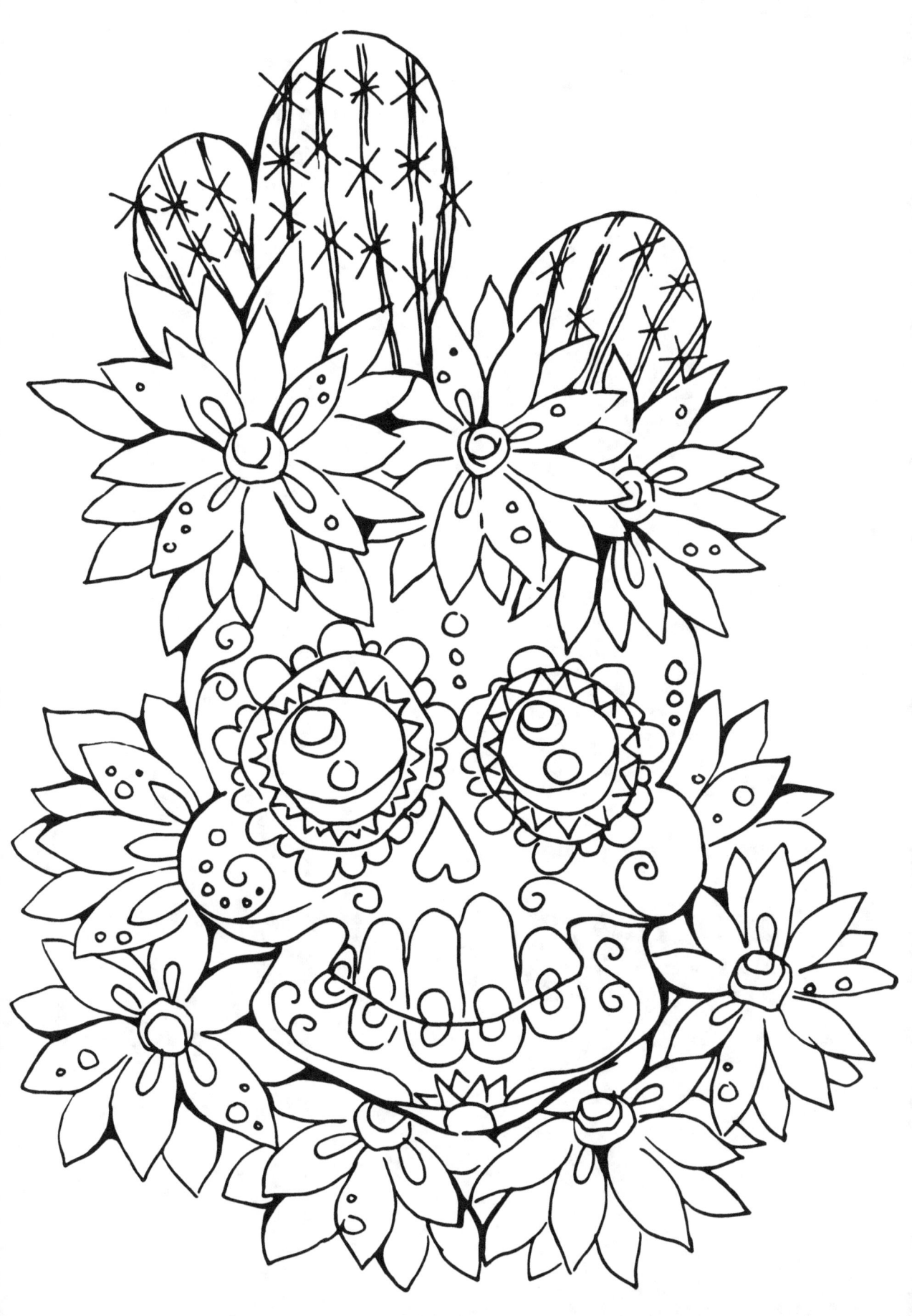

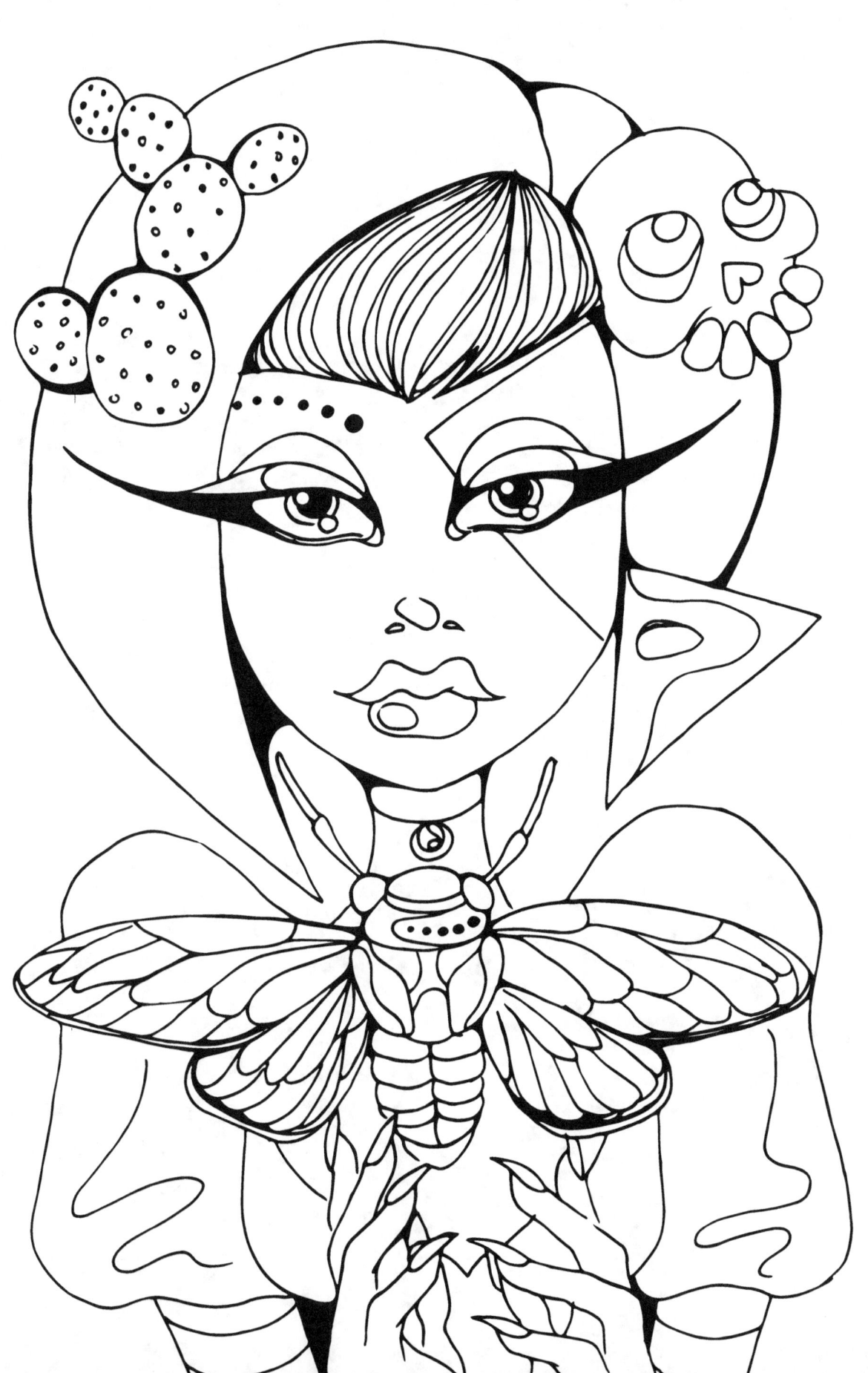

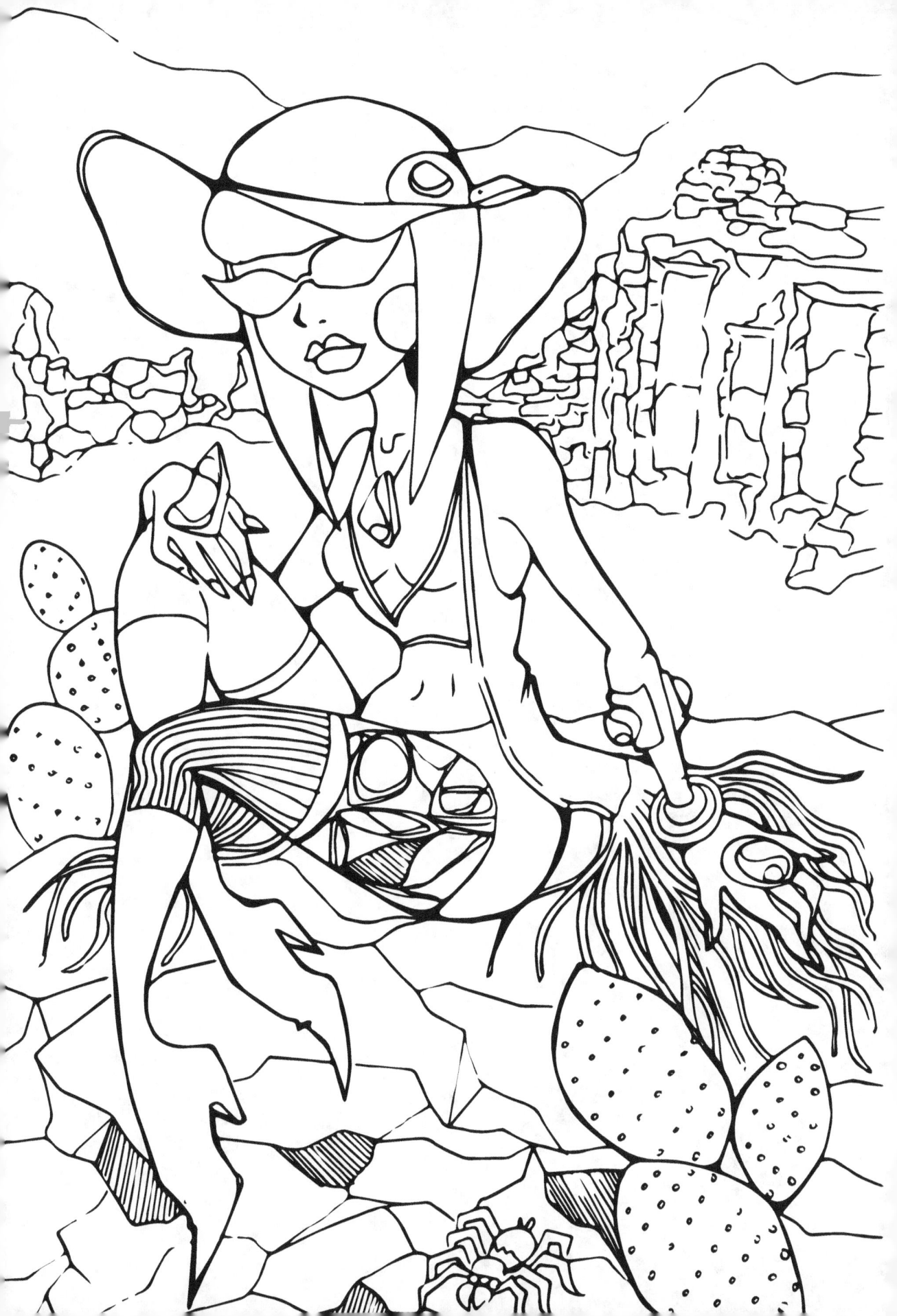

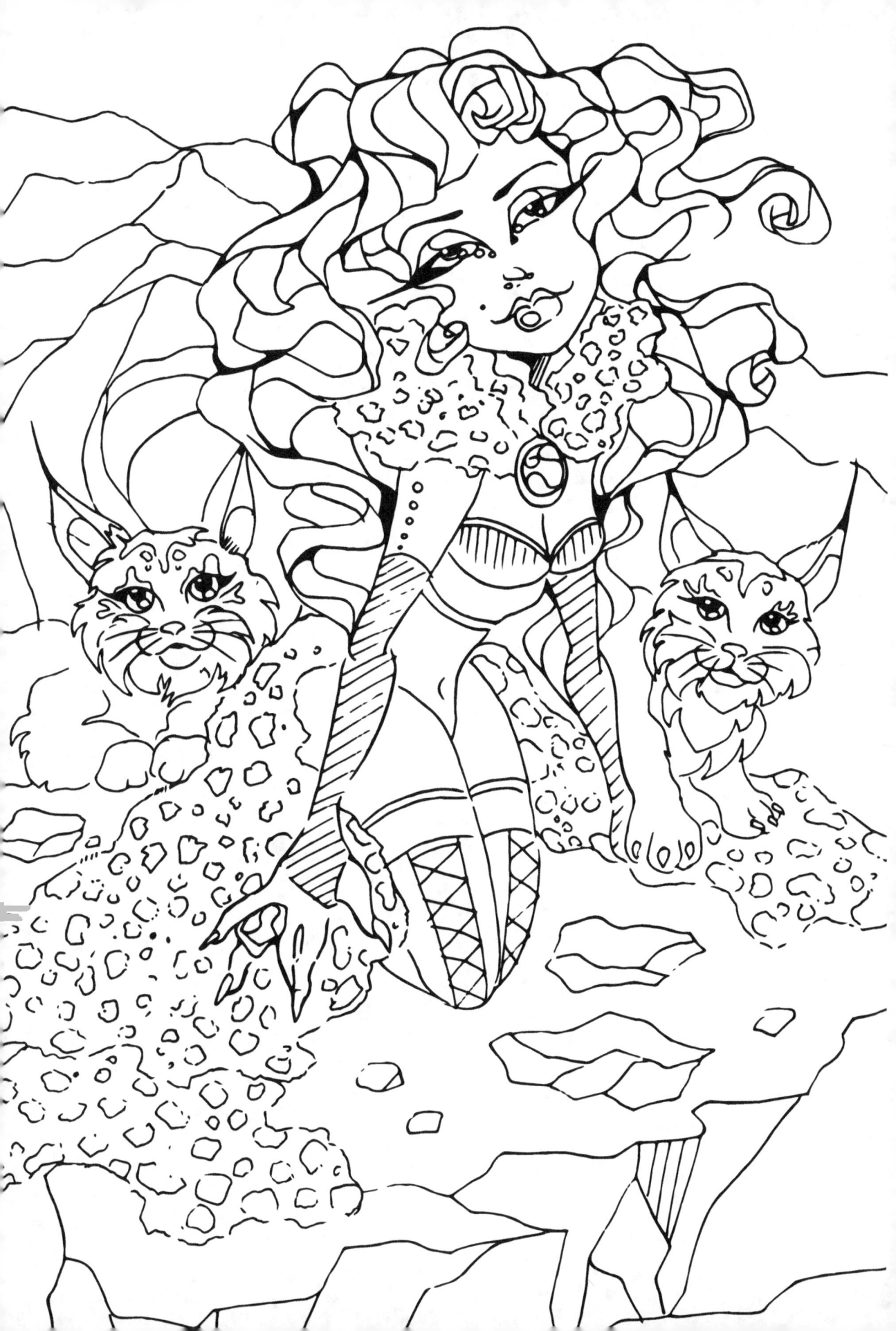

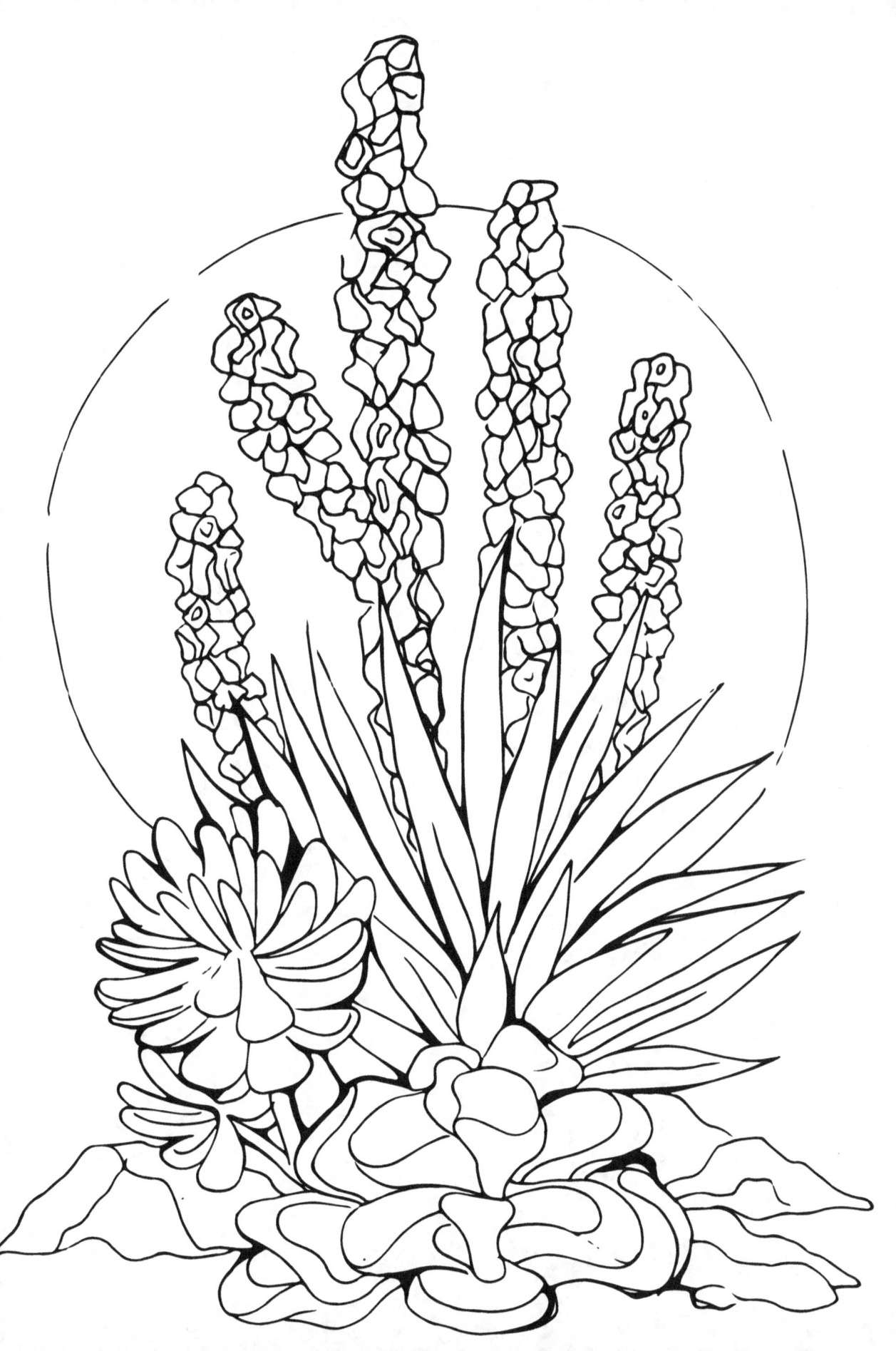

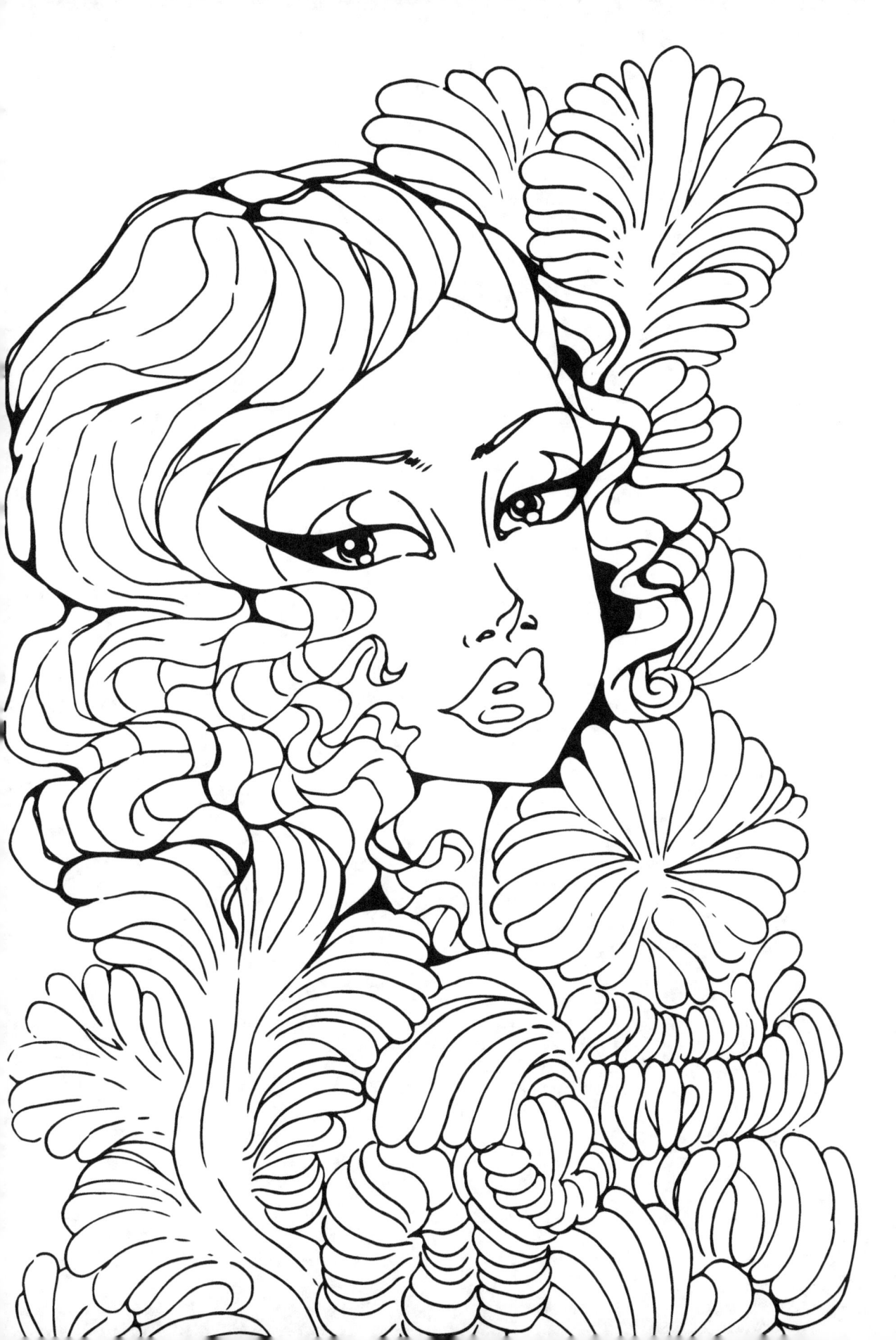

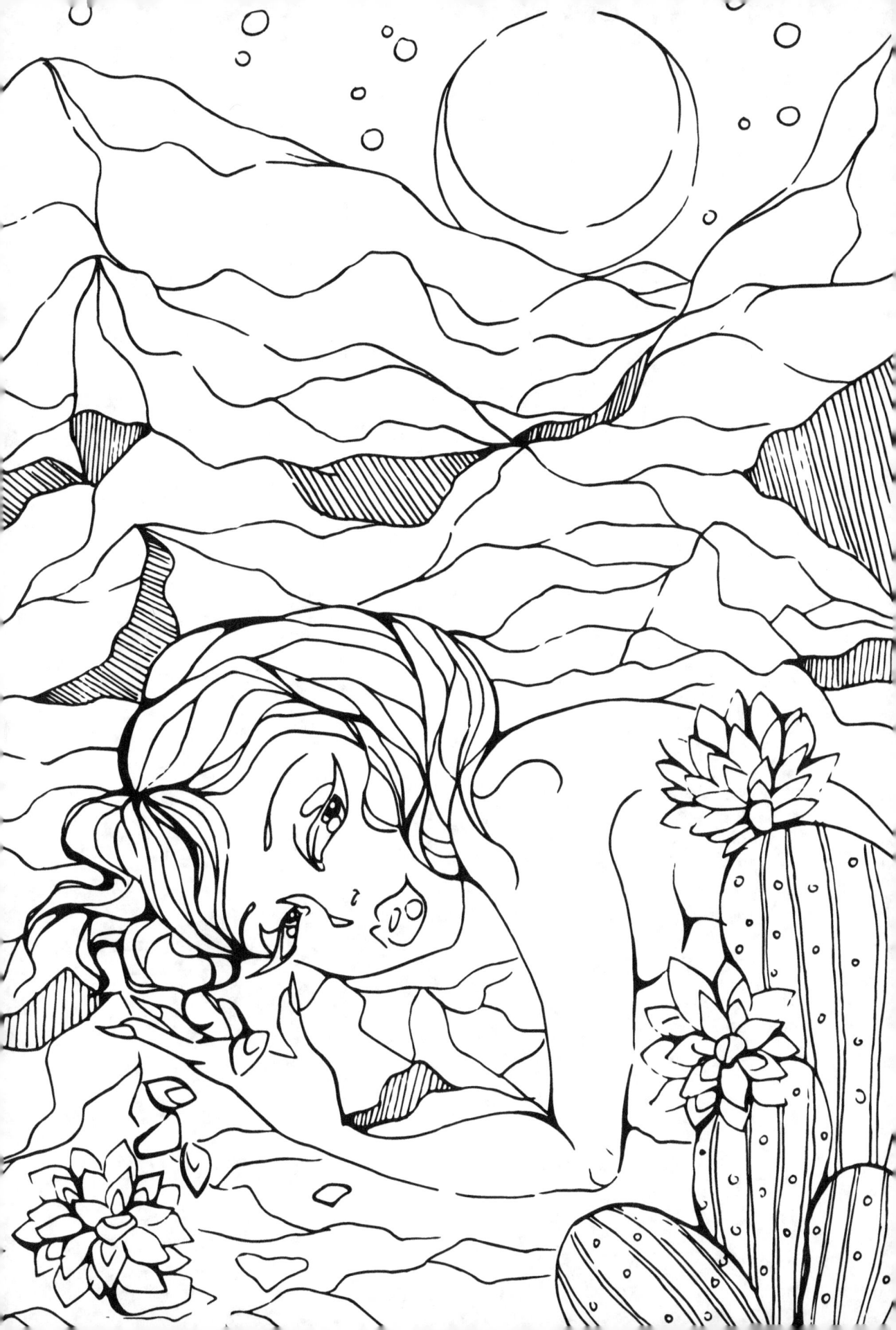

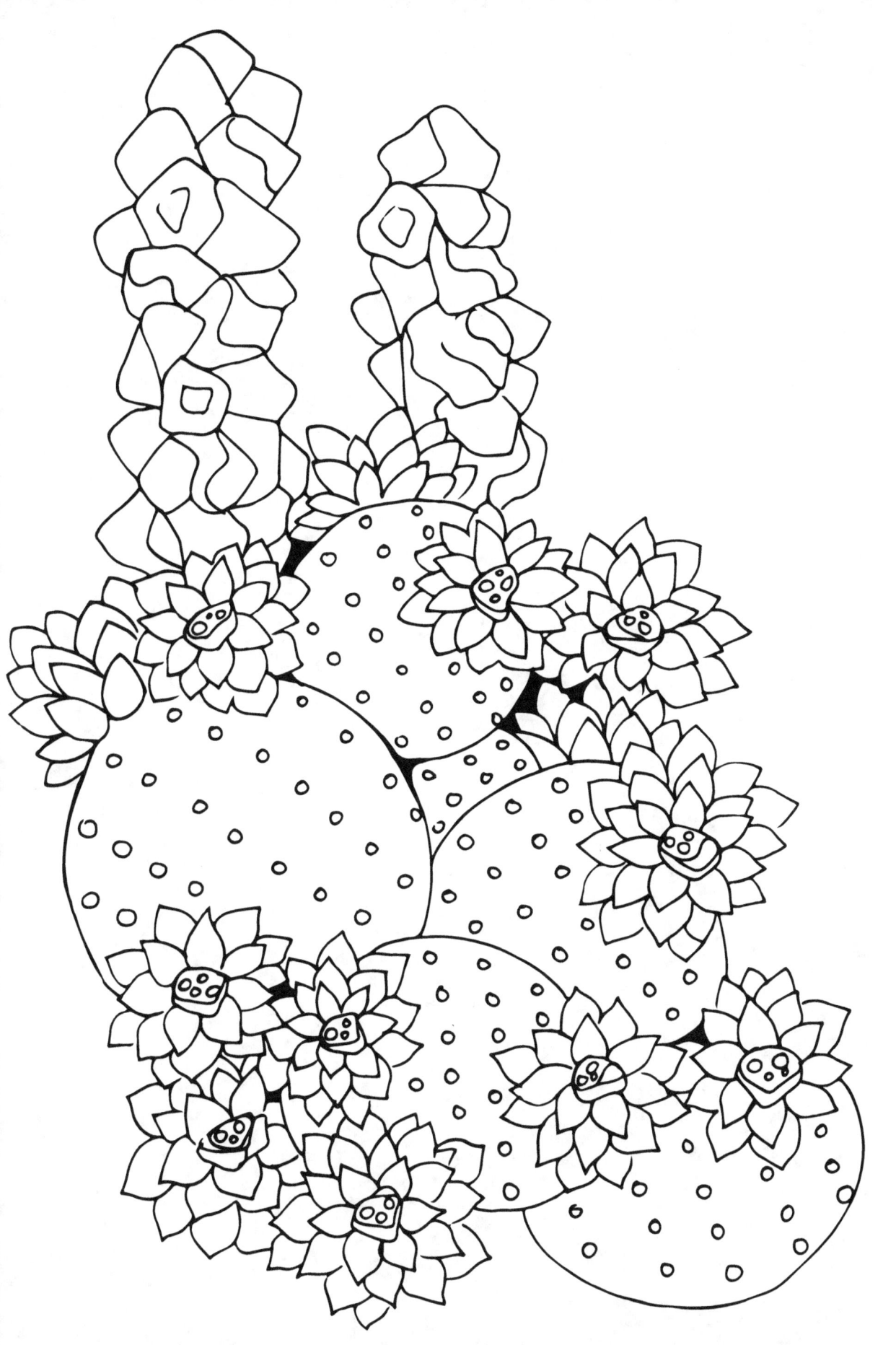

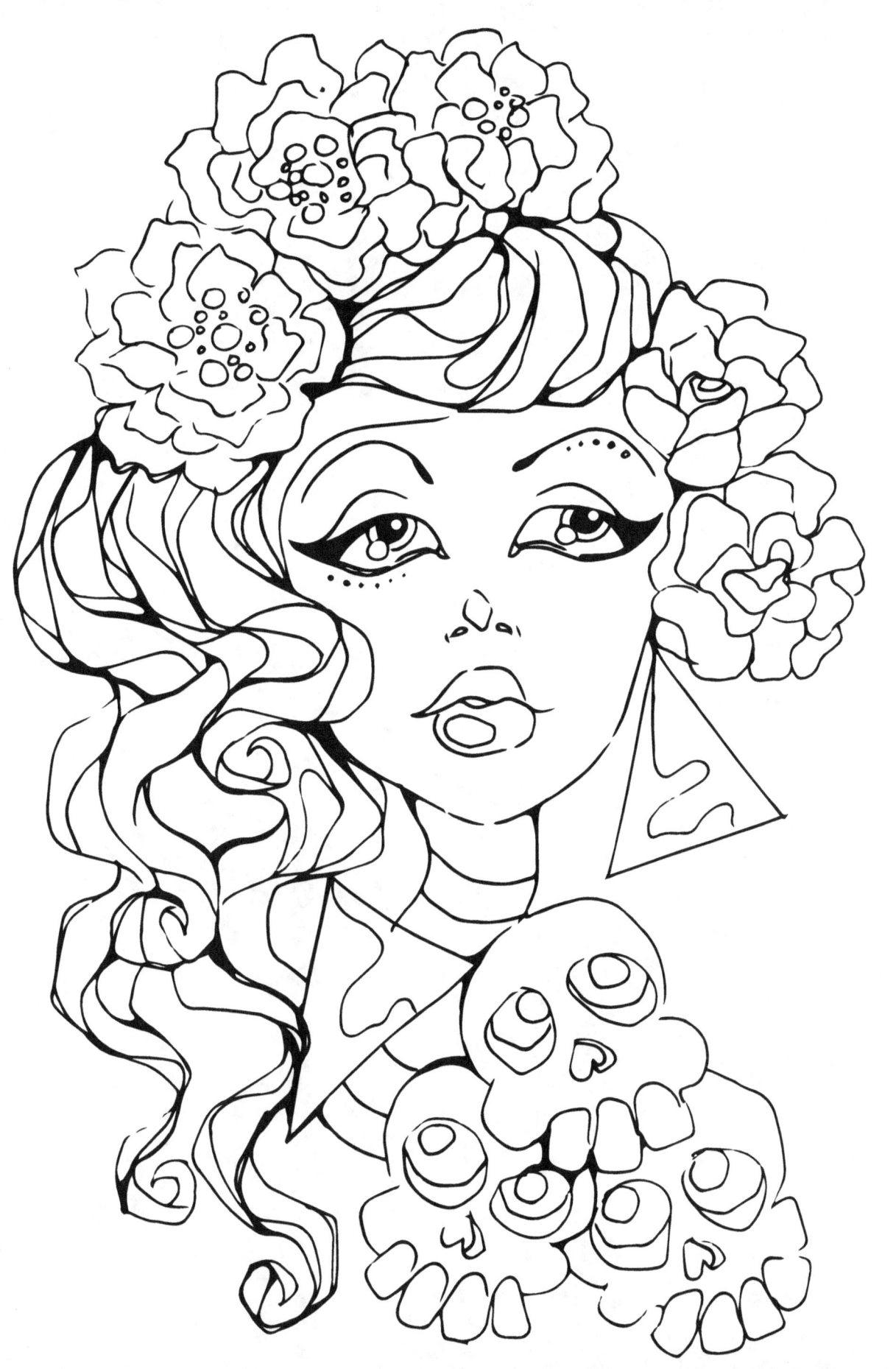

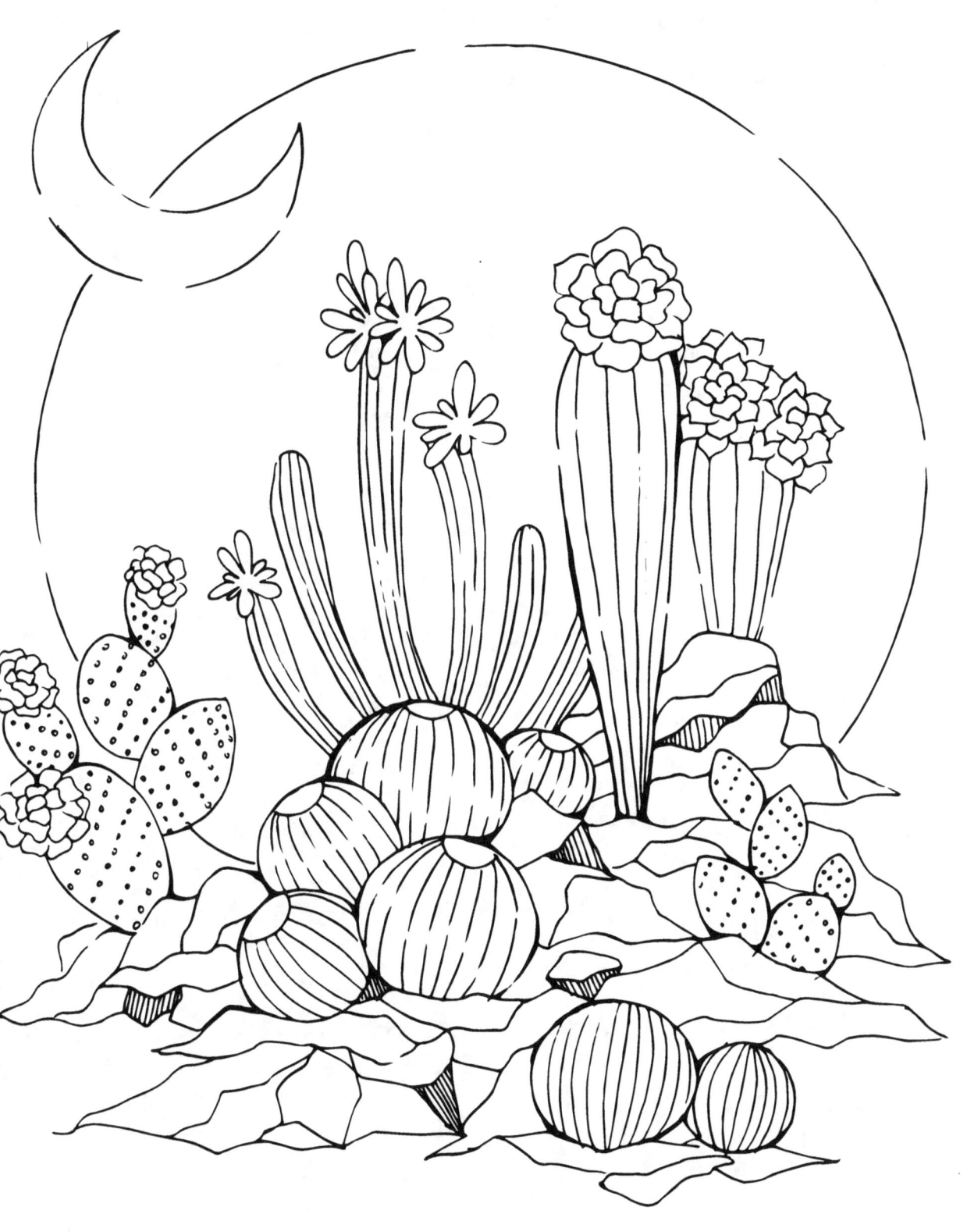

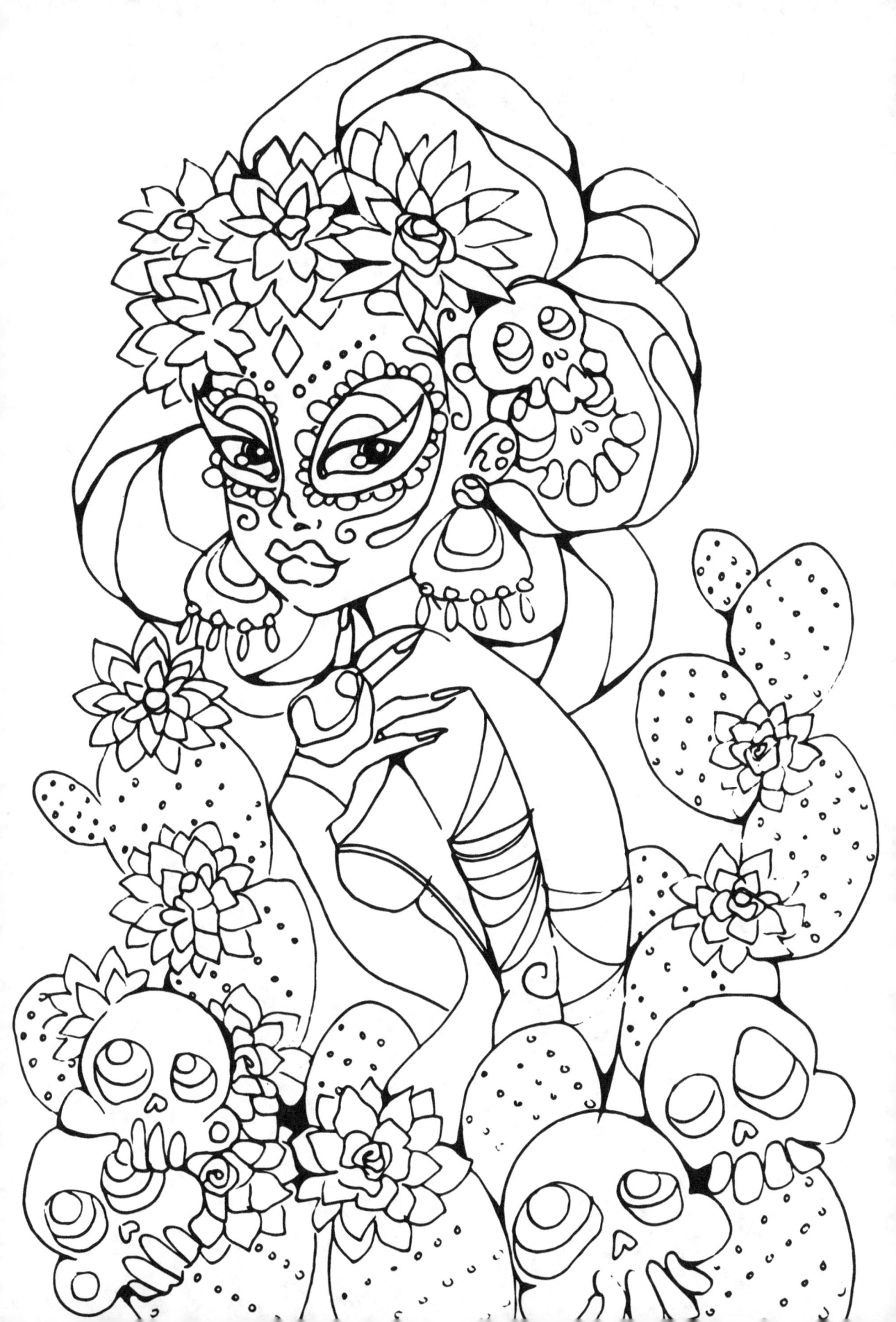

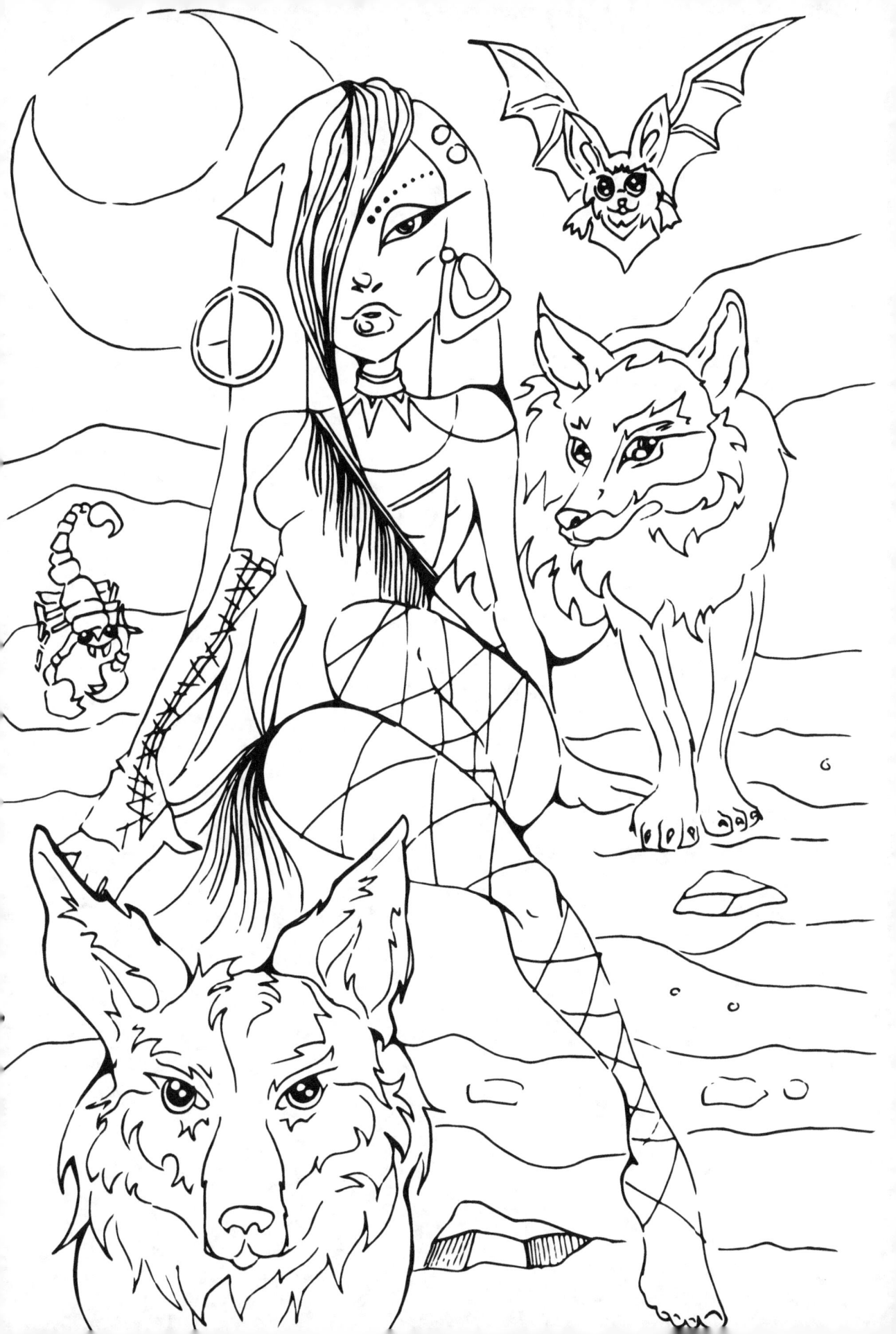

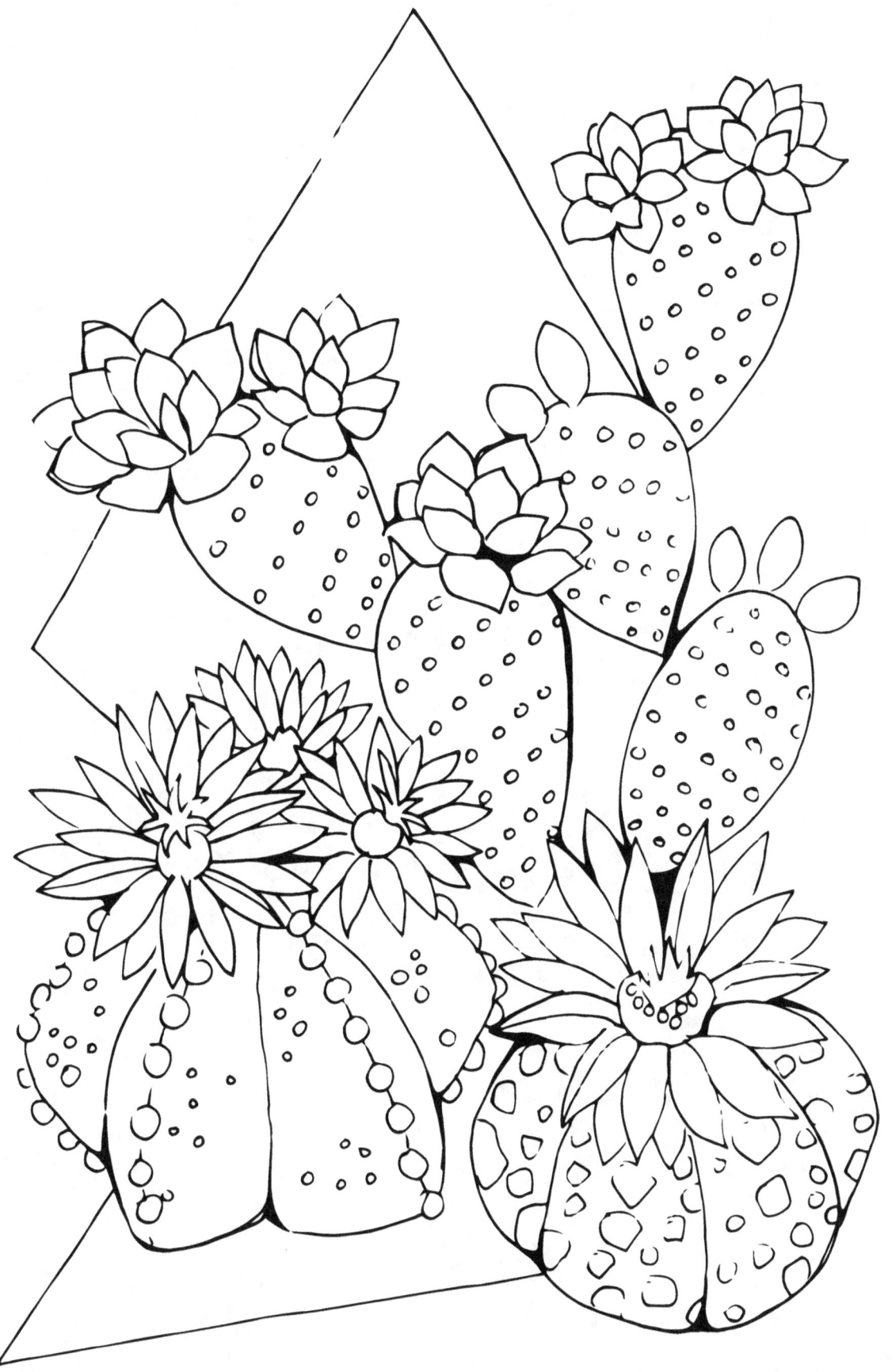

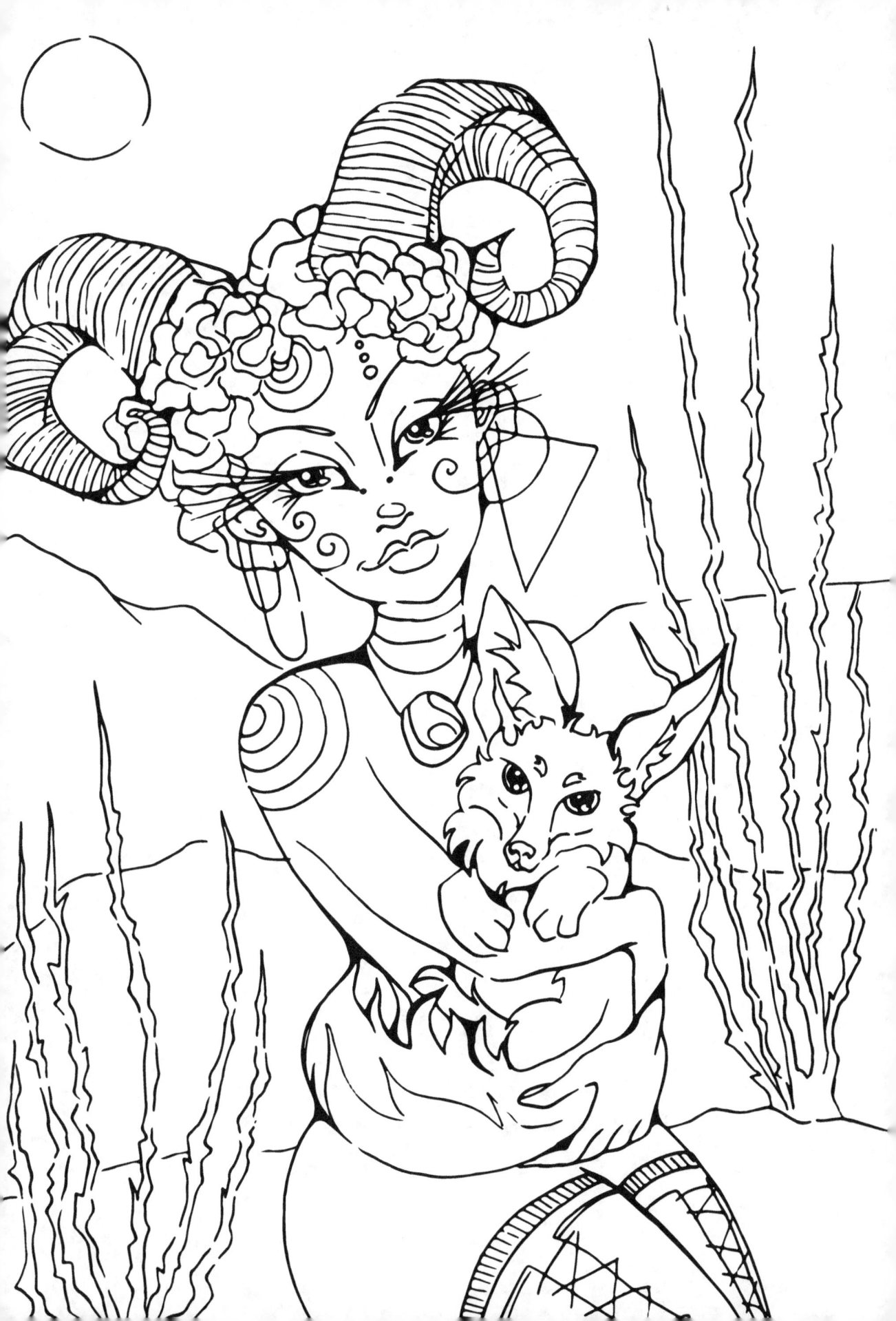

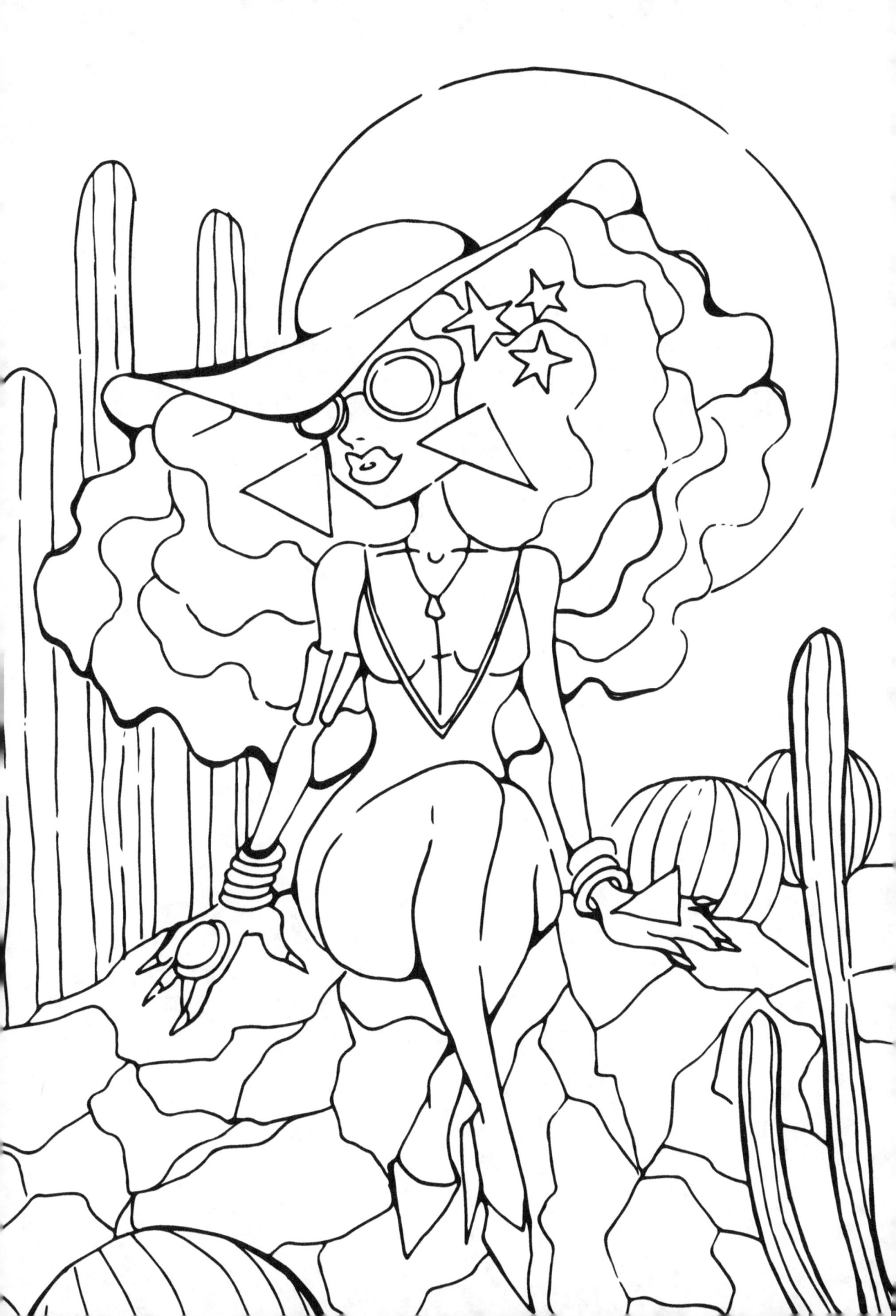

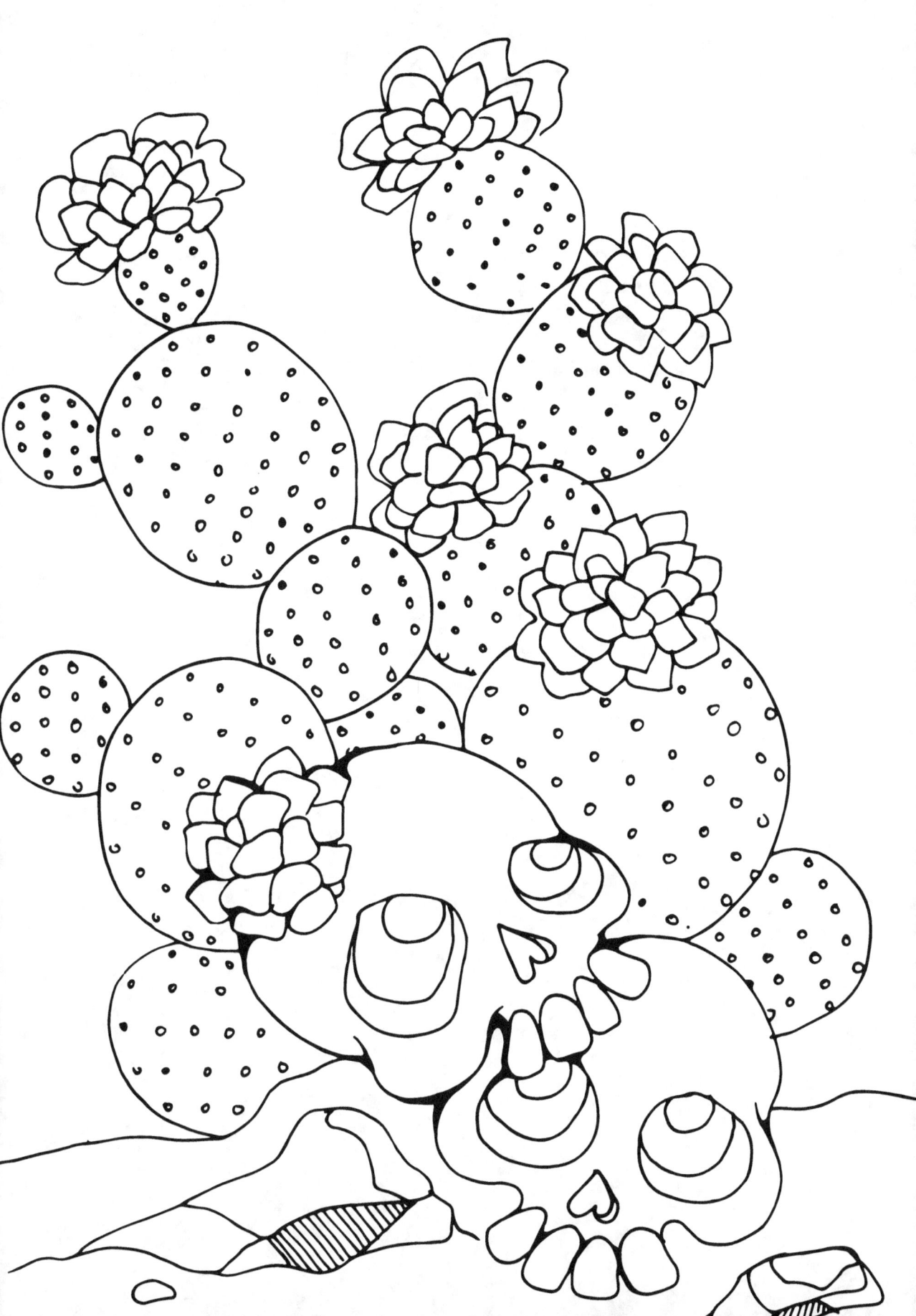

TESTER PAGE

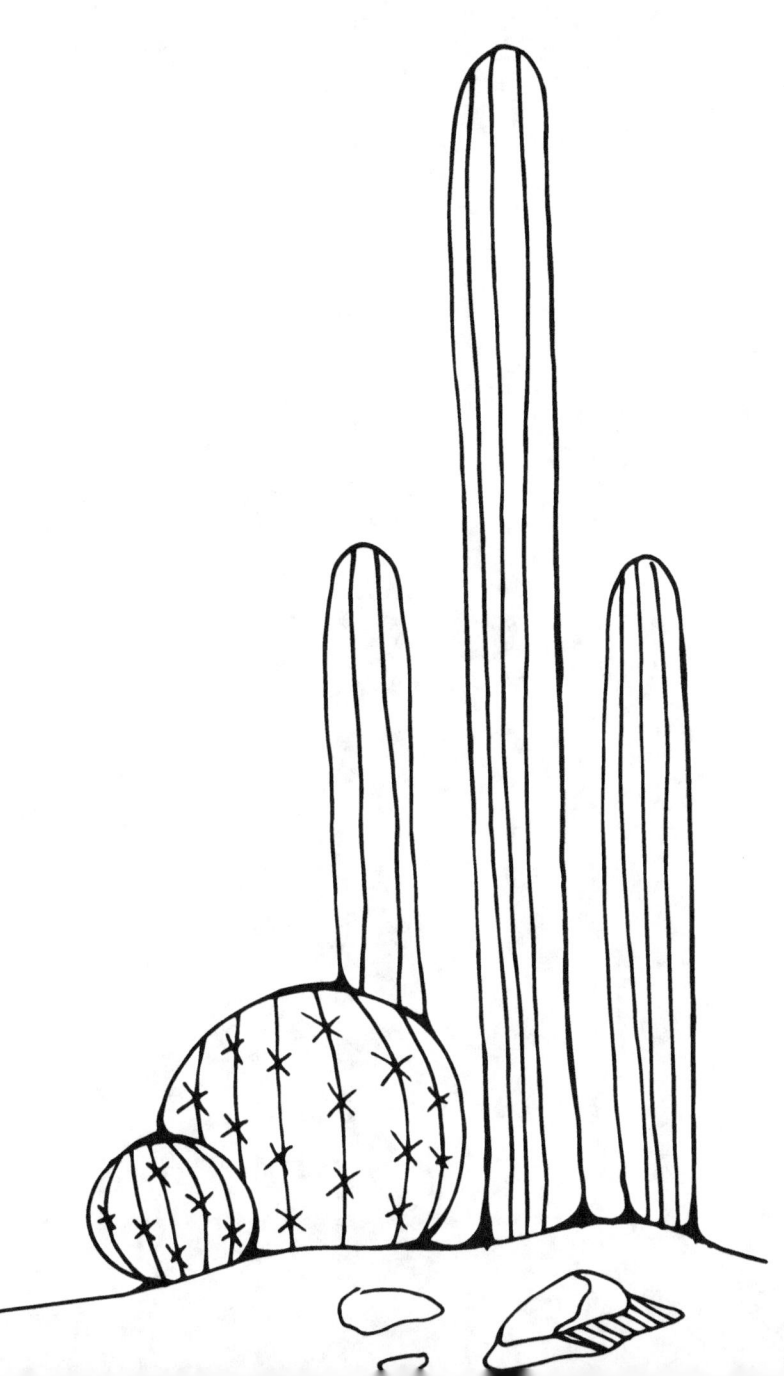

TESTER PAGE

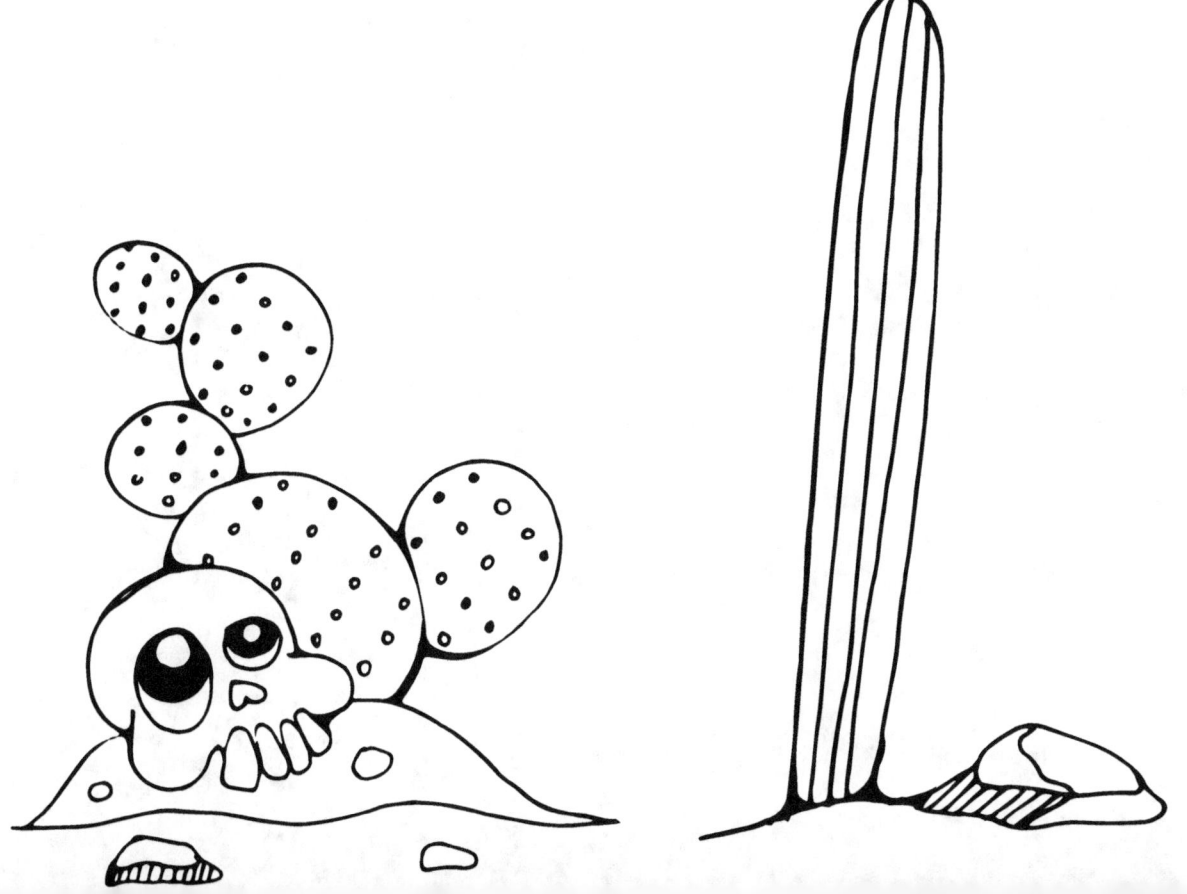

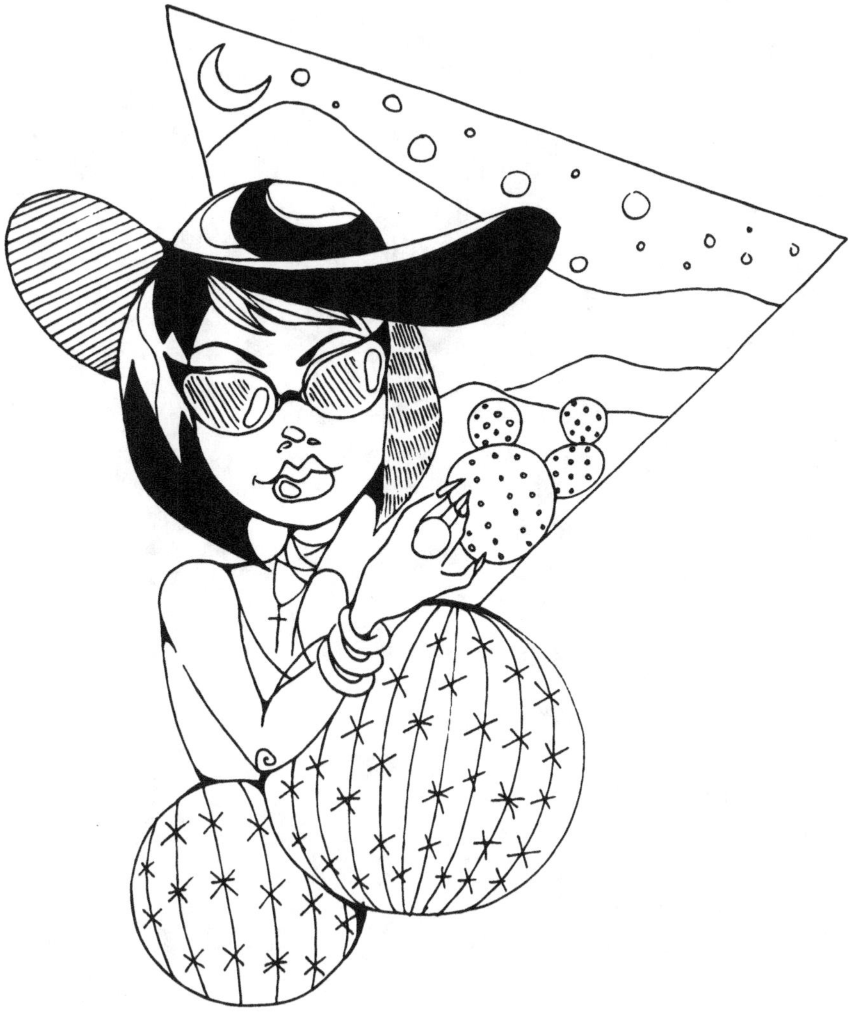

MY HOME, MY MUSE
I dedicate this book to the desert.

JOIN ME ONLINE

FACEBOOK | artistkarlamagana
INSTAGRAM | karla_magana

#desertmusecoloringbook
to share your pages!

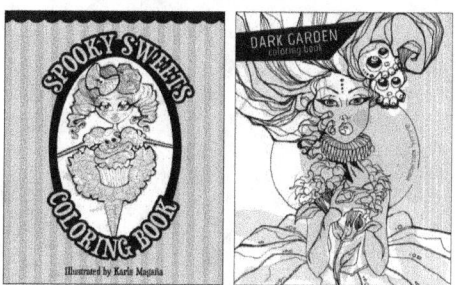
KARLAMAGANA.COM